UNCONDITIONAL ENERGY HEALING

Published in 2022 by David Bateman Ltd,
Unit 2/5 Workspace Drive, Hobsonville,
Auckland 0618, New Zealand
www.batemanbooks.co.nz

ISBN: 978-1-77689-022-4

A catalogue record for this book is available from the National Library of New Zealand.

Book design: Nick Turzynski, redinc. Book Design, www.redinc.co.nz
Photography and images: 12, 22, 26, 32, 36, 38, 60, 65, 78, 80, 83, 91, 94, 95, 103, 112, 116, 127, 137, 138, 140, 151, 154, 157, 159, 161, 167, 169, 171, 176, 179, 182, 187, 189, 191, 198, 200 via Canva.com; 31, 51, 62, 63, 98, 99, 107, 175 created by Kawika Design; 119, 194, 198 from Pexels.com; all other images used are public domain.

Printed in China by Toppan Leefung Printing Ltd

UNCONDITIONAL ENERGY HEALING

The effortless self-healing method

BRETT ELLIOTT

BATEMAN BOOKS

Contents

Preface

After a single healing session: regular epileptic fits completely stopped; a baby conceived after years of failed attempts; long-term wart suddenly falls off; anxiety and depression resolved; a rash disappears overnight; and chronic back pain gone instantly. These are just a few cases of Unconditional Energy Healing in action.

If only there was a 'holy grail' of self-healing that was so easy and simple that anyone could do it. After all, the simplest answer is most often correct, so why would healing be any different? The biggest issue we face in the world today is complexity. Life has become too complicated, especially healthcare.

Over 22 years of clinical practice, I have reached more than 100,000 people in more than 45 countries with my health programmes, which have cured many of the most common health conditions of our time. I started researching natural medicine in the mid 1990s when I realised, purely by accident, that I had a healing gift.

Years later, while studying biophysics and human physiology at university, a scientific explanation for healing started coming together. I developed a healing technique that I now teach to my clients individually and in groups. Here in this book I share this healing technique with you.

You will gain an understanding of what 'unconditional healing energy' actually is and learn how to connect with and channel this infinite energy to heal yourself and others. The method is outlined in simple clear diagrams using scientific principles. This allows you to obtain personal experiences of the healing energy and then direct it to heal your body, emotions and even your mind. The possibilities are almost limitless!

Introduction

If DNA can store millions of times more information per gram than our most advanced computer storage devices, and reproduce itself without outside intervention, which no computer can do, then who are we to claim that it randomly formed all by itself, as what we call 'evolution'? Science today would have us believe it was an accident in a pool of mud and was the first molecule in the development of all life on the planet. It's a very bold claim to make, and almost naïve when you really take some time to think about it. The scientific community needs to take another look.

On the flip side, innate universal intelligence can be seen everywhere when you begin looking at things deeply enough. A caterpillar can turn into a butterfly and a tadpole into a frog within only a few short days. They are transforming into entirely different creatures, growing new limbs, and completely changing in shape and size. This is all down to pre-programmed DNA code. Just like a computer memory chip, any new information can potentially be coded and stored in DNA. The DNA in your body alone could store all the digital information mankind has ever created. In the near future we will certainly be using synthetic DNA as computer memory. Can we be programmed without our knowing, or even reprogramme ourselves deliberately, and can our DNA actually receive new 'more advanced' information from beyond the physical realm, for healing?

Do we have the power to tap into innate universal intelligence and if so, what are the rules and guidelines? How will we know when we are actually doing this and what will it look, sound, and feel like? Read on and discover the answers to all of these questions.

Seekers throughout the ages appear to have found universal intelligent energy and developed healing arts of various modalities, but with the knowledge we have today of physics, the cosmos, communication systems and the human body there must surely be a modern, more generic, scientific way of seeing the process of self-healing with energy? There is such a method, and it's called Unconditional Energy Healing. Unconditional means it's just there, regardless of what you do, think or say; it is not going anywhere and will not change. It's always the same regardless of conditions, a bit like gravity or our sun.

In recent decades our technology has advanced rapidly, to the point where we can now scan our bodies with electromagnetic devices, see into the depths of space, live stream instantly around the globe, and even manipulate the human genome.

But with all of this advanced technology, we still appear unable to cure some of the most prevalent health conditions such as the flu, common digestive complaints, mental health issues, chronic fatigue, and epidemics of metabolic, hormonal and autoimmune disease.

The simple fact is that modern science often begets narrow-mindedness. In other words, the young scientist can sometimes become so awed by science and tangled up in specialist details, that they forget that science itself has only understood a very small fraction of our reality, our cosmos, and ourselves as human beings. Potentially under 1 per cent.

Things currently unknown to science include:

- over 90 per cent of the cosmos, including dark energy, dark matter, infinite size, and the beginning of time[1]
- how the universe began, i.e. the Big Bang theory is still a theory, full of holes and unproven
- how life itself actually began, a complete mystery[2]

- human consciousness — what it is and where it is exactly, and how does it operate?[3]
- the true nature of human dreams and the ability to record our actual thoughts, emotions (feelings) and love
- 99 per cent of intestinal human bacteria still unknown[4]
- 80 per cent of the ocean floor, still unexplored[5]
- God (creation), spirituality, and belief in the existence of life after death, to which over 84 per cent of humans subscribe.

As you can see, science does not fully understand the nature of human perception itself. We do not understand the basic biochemical mechanisms of some of our most common experiences, such as the many human aspects of creativity, imagination, out-of-body, or dream states. This is also true for extraordinary states of consciousness such as 'visions' or phenomena such as near-death experiences.

These things are crucial to understanding the energy of the universe; the source of life itself; human consciousness and spirituality. Understanding the biochemical mechanisms behind these common experiences may help us discover the causes and cures for many diseases. Otherwise, we are just poking and prodding at our bodies with our blunt and primitive methods.

The drugs, surgeries and drastic and expensive interventions are not keeping people healthy, but instead patching us up, a temporary fix. We don't have healthcare systems; we have what should be called 'disease-care systems' — doctors are trained in treating disease, not in deeply understanding health. We need to properly understand the nature of holistic health and the healing process, and yet this is not on many governments' agendas.

The problem with modern science

Scientists often forget that the greatest minds that ever lived, and the grandfathers of modern science, such as Albert Einstein and Isaac Newton, originally set out on a quest to prove their belief/theory that there was a great intelligence behind the scenes designing the universe. They postulated that if this was correct then everything should follow distinct, intelligent laws and rational mathematical principles. Without such intelligent design a chaotic, disorderly universe would otherwise certainly have manifested, and without intelligent intervention, a prehistoric pool of warm liquid would have remained a pool of warm liquid forever, end of story. Everything these two geniuses set out to prove has since been found to be correct, and their discoveries formed the backbone of what we now call 'modern science'.

Einstein acknowledged that his own understanding of God was rooted in his belief in a supreme intelligence underpinning the universe.[6] **Newton** believed that behind the veil of the physical world lived a divine, infinite intelligence that continuously supported and maintained it. The God who designed the universe and the life it hosts was infinitely superior to the human ability to understand Him. Newton saw himself 'like a boy playing on the seashore, and diverting myself by now and then finding a smoother pebble or a prettier shell than ordinary, whilst the great ocean of truth lay all undiscovered before me'.[7] This kind of genuine intellectual humility is found among the greatest scientific minds.

Through their discoveries, research, and experimentation Einstein and Newton both found their theories to be true, revealing layer upon layer of intelligent design hidden within the structure and behaviour of our universe. Yet science today broadly claims there is no evidence for a universal intelligence and that everything has inadvertently happened by chance, random occurrence, natural selection, accidental mutation or coincidence.

This couldn't be further from the truth, because to this day, Einstein and Newton are revered as having uncovered the ultimate secrets to how the universe operates from predictable, incontrovertible governing laws. In other words, the evidence for intelligent design is absolutely everywhere we look — that is, if you're really looking for it.

There does appear to be a large number of scientists who are suffering what I call 'scientific blindness', a form of narrow-mindedness that leaves them with many blank spaces in the text books that can never be filled until infinite universal intelligence is recognised.

The 'atheistic scientist' view may in fact underlie many problems we face in the world today, especially within our medical and healthcare systems. Putting our faith entirely in our limited science, man-made drugs, and medical interventions is a false solution to our worldwide health crises when traditional long-term holistic healing is what we need as human beings.

Don't get me wrong. I love science, and we have seen huge positive impacts on our standard of living due to modern science. What I propose is that we keep our present level of knowledge in perspective, allowing for infinitely more to be discovered, especially when it comes to those 'currently unknown' areas just mentioned.

Ironically, approximately 50 per cent of scientists still claim to have a religious or spiritual faith. Do evolution and creation both have common-sense explanations when you allow for the possibility of infinite time, infinite space, and infinite intelligence? Of course they do. It's called intelligent design. Why should it be any different when it comes to our health?

The true scientist keeps an open mind and realises the limitations of current knowledge. The true scientist is an explorer of new theories and performs many experiments. The true scientist is an adventurer into the unknown. They assume nothing, hold an attitude of humility, and make no conclusions without first employing rigorous testing, with an unbiased analysis of the results.

Let the journey begin

I invite you to be like this type of scientist and join me on a journey of self-discovery and realisation. No matter where you are along your own healing path, I invite you to experiment with this new healing method, test and measure your results and take note of your experiences as you embark on this healing pilgrimage.

In this book, I will share with you the secrets of energy healing, which have been revealed to me over 25 years of energy healing within my private practice. I will give you simple methods that you can test immediately, and practical explanations, using scientific principles, including references along the way.

I will start by explaining the nature of healing energy, where it comes from, and how it moves; then I will explain how you can tune in, connect with it, and channel it. Ultimately you should have direct experiences of healing energy within yourself that can bring you immediate and measurable results.

Lastly, I will give you the secrets to tap into an infinite supply of this healing energy and encourage it to penetrate every part of your body, heart and mind to fill you with happiness and peace. You will not only be able to heal yourself but potentially help others to do the same.

I know this all sounds too good to be true, but I assure you it's possible. All it takes is an open mind, some experimentation, practice and perseverance.

Prepare to experience more within yourself than you imagined possible.

PART ONE

UNDERSTANDING UNCONDITIONAL HEALING ENERGY

Chapter 1:

A higher perspective

I'm going to start by explaining how to put yourself in the right space to connect with and receive unconditional healing energy. By this I mean a mental space, point of view, or perspective. This entails putting aside your past understandings and allowing for a new paradigm, a new, expanded view of the world and of yourself. Prepare to get out of your head and experience your infinite nature.

For each of us, our life on earth started with a clean slate. Our memory of anything prior to this life had been wiped away. We were pure, open, unblemished and innocent. This didn't last long. We immediately started to experience pain, discomfort and emotional, mental stressors. It's these painful experiences in life and our reactions that can let us down.

To cope with these difficult experiences as we go through life, we develop opinions, attitudes and beliefs, all based on our surroundings, our family, culture, society, language, and personal and professional relationships. A large proportion of these opinions, attitudes, and beliefs are defence mechanisms, and these do not necessarily represent true knowledge in scientific terms. In fact, these ideas we develop largely constitute a fabrication and don't often truly serve to benefit us, especially in the long-term.

Our experiences in life build our character and personality. This character and personality, or self-identity, is known in Freudian theory as our 'ego', and is built upon by these experiences. In this context, our ego is made from our experience-based personality, with its opinions, beliefs and attitudes.[2]

It is important to identify the distinct difference between our ego's opinions, attitudes and beliefs, and actual knowledge, and our true deeper eternal nature. In order to obtain true knowledge and a new understanding of something profound enough to heal our body and mind, we need to get outside and above these self-constructed unrealities and this limited self-identity/ego.

We need to burst our bubble, think outside the box, transcend our physical boundaries and allow a new level of universal consciousness to distil in us.

Rising above = transcending

I know this may seem challenging, but in order to take on the pure energy and healing available, it is very important to take a higher perspective than we may have had until now.

We must attain the highest possible perspective in order to truly heal ourselves. Similar to how we drive a vehicle, or how a jockey controls a horse, we must realise our limited, worldly, self-constructed ego is controlling us, and break free from it in order to become attuned to the place where healing energy resides. Then we can truly tap into an infinite healing power.

In order to be released, or to break free from the limiting patterns of our past, we need to transcend them, so we can take control with a new, higher universal knowledge. After all, knowledge is power, right?

Could you operate surgically on your own heart and perform a triple bypass? I don't think so. You need somebody else who is above and beyond the limitations of your body to perform the surgery for you.

Can you easily solve a maze and find the exit without knowing the design or seeing the plan from above? No, but if you could have a bird's-eye view of the maze you would easily walk right out without a wrong turn.

The biggest problem we face when trying to heal ourselves is this very principle. It's hard to rise above our past patterns, engrained attitudes, beliefs, opinions and even our current situations and circumstances. It's a bit like we are a puppet on a string sometimes, under the control of our subconscious ego, with its limited beliefs, opinions, attitudes and the reactionary coping mechanisms it has inflicted upon us.

A perfect example of how to achieve higher self-control is found by describing the interplay between the three major levels of ourselves, namely: the physical, the emotional and the mental.

Physical: the body

For us to heal our body physically we cannot be under the power of our body's basic impulses, addictive appetites and desires, which means we must rise above the carnal, animalistic physical body by taking control of our emotions. The keywords here are 'rise above', but this emotional discipline can be a struggle in itself.

Emotional: our feelings

In order for us to take control of our emotions, we must 'rise above' them and take the reins, by using the power of our mind. It is futile attempting to heal and balance ourselves emotionally without first gaining some mental self-control. After all, who should be driving this vehicle anyway?

Mental: our mind

This can be a runaway train if we're not behind the controls. To truly

and effectively heal ourselves mentally, we must enlighten our minds, and gain knowledge of things above and beyond our previous worldly experiences. Yes, we must also rise above the mind, but in particular, the personal ego-based mind, and even the collective society-based subconscious 'super-ego' or 'group think'.[3] We must tap into and realise a higher form of awareness called 'universal consciousness.' But how can we do this?

Astronauts talk about a shift in consciousness that occurs when they first travel to space and see the earth from above. It's called the overview effect.[4] It is the experience of seeing first-hand the reality of the earth in space, which is immediately perceived differently and understood to be a tiny, fragile ball of life, 'hanging in the void', protected and nourished by a paper-thin atmosphere. From space, national boundaries vanish, the conflicts that divide people become insignificant, and the need to create a planetary society with the united will to protect this 'pale blue dot' becomes both obvious and imperative. This effect is a very common experience and has occurred with many astronauts.[1] You may have had a version of this yourself from an aeroplane.

Consider a place above and beyond language, culture, race, nation and even our world. A place where all absolute knowledge resides and where healing and a culmination of all universal consciousness and infinite energy reside.

Consider a place beyond our physical world, where heavy physical matter ceases to exist and everything is in a pure-energy state. This is

a place where we no longer have the worldly boundaries that exist on earth or in the physical realm. This is the place of our dreams, a place of pure consciousness and energy. This is the place we need to connect with and directly experience as tangible and real, in order to accomplish Unconditional Energy Healing.

The healing energy that comes from this place of universal or collective cosmic consciousness does not follow the same rules as our past experiences here on earth. For us to truly connect with and receive healing we must aspire to this higher place. For the sake of this text, we will call it 'a higher perspective'.

Once there, we have the potential to connect with and tap into the healing energy. We will talk about this process of rising above, tuning in, and tapping into healing energy in more detail in coming chapters.

For now, please take some time to consider and ponder deeply this 'higher perspective' concept, and what that perspective may look and feel like for you. You will be needing it in order to continue forward on this healing journey.

I strongly advise taking a few minutes right now to sit, close your eyes and breathe slowly, allowing this idea to permeate your mind so you can tune in to the feelings it brings.

In the next chapter I will talk about how the healing energy actually moves.

My personal story begins . . .

As a very young child of only two and half years old I can remember having a couple of experiences that I will never forget. In every child the mind is wide open and there are no filters, so you can begin to imagine/see things. I can clearly remember going to an outdoor toilet at night. As I walked out to the toilet, which was only a few steps from the back door, I would see moving shapes and shadows that resembled monsters to me. They were so vivid that I could not go out the door without my

father. For many years I was also haunted by nightmares that were most peculiar. The strangest was the dream where I would wake up, get out of bed and wander out into the main living area of the house. There I was confronted by my parents, who had the faces of wolves. I would begin to scream and not be able to wake up. I later found out from my parents that this recurring dream involved me sleepwalking around the house with my eyes open. Another common recurring dream as a teenager was one of flying. I would fly over the country, the mountains and sometimes the world. These dreams were so vivid they seemed almost real in the morning. These dreams happened less and less as I got older.

The reason I am sharing these experiences is to demonstrate the difference between the mind of a child and that of an adult. As we get older we tend to block out these types of experiences, as we form a more structured view of the world and inevitably construct mental and emotional filters. The more we can adopt an innocent, childlike, open-minded view, the more we can experience our true higher nature and awareness.

Chapter 2:

Energy exchange

I call the healing method detailed in this book Unconditional Energy Healing. This method is well supported by the laws of our universe. These laws are set in motion from the very foundation of creation and do not change according to human behaviour. Gravity and sunshine are great examples. They don't care if you are rich or poor, black or white, male or female, or whether you have been good or bad in the past. Gravity and sunshine are unconditional, but if you don't understand how they operate, or try to go against them, you will suffer the consequences. Likewise, healing energy follows universal laws, it's unconditional, and similarly, if we don't comprehend those laws we suffer. All we need to do is understand these laws, and then we can use this unconditional energy to heal. I will be talking a lot about these universal laws throughout this book.

The first law of physics is the 'law of conservation', which states that 'Energy can neither be created nor destroyed; rather, it transforms from one form to another.'[1] To expand on this we could say that 'energy simply moves from one place to another', whether that is into another energy form, molecular form, or into another medium.

To demonstrate this, let's explore how we generate electricity. We simply capture the energy of gravity in a dam and run water through turbines, or we capture the kinetic energy of the wind or the heat from coal to run a turbine; or we capture sunlight converting the heat and light into electrical power.

That power is then used to charge batteries, heat homes and run appliances, etc. All this energy eventually returns back to the universe as heat, even if this takes billions of years.[2] The fact remains: energy is never lost, it simply moves around, changes form and is endlessly recycled. It is conserved. A similar example of this energy law is found in diffusion, which you can see in the diagram below.

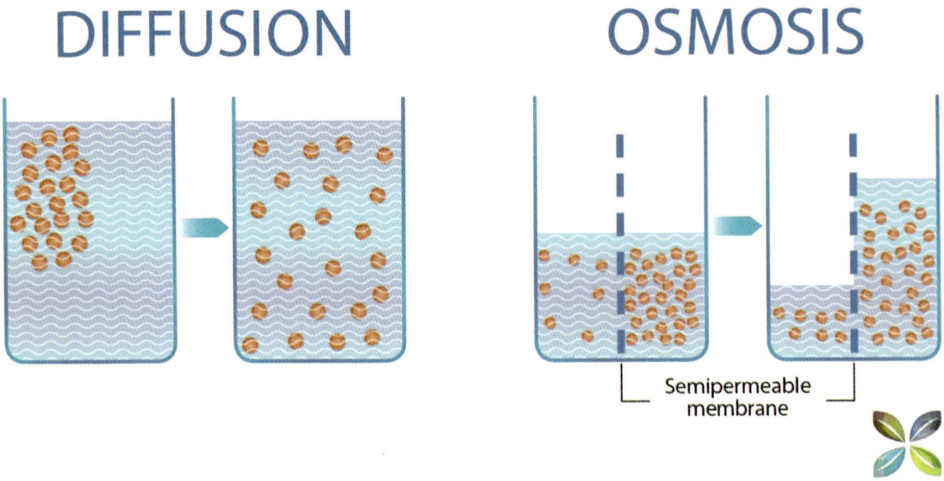

The example of diffusion shows how a substance let loose into a liquid or a gas will spread out and fill the entire space evenly, a bit like a bad smell in a room or a teaspoon of sugar in your cup of tea. You could also say this happens when we eat something, think something or apply the knowledge of a principle into our lives. That energy is never lost, it just spreads out evenly within us. To expand on this energy conservation concept, let's pose another question: How much energy do we actually have available?

Osmosis might help answer this. The law of osmosis usually applies to water and it means that water will move through a membrane to balance the concentration of a substance in the water. This happens a lot with salts and acids in our bodies because salt and acid balance is crucial to stay alive. Osmosis is more to do with equilibrium than the conservation of energy, but the energy principle is similar because energy simply moves and is never lost.

Supposing that healing energy might come from an infinite universal source, it's always there, just waiting for an opportunity to move our way. Therefore similar energy laws must apply to how healing energy moves.

Remember that energy is never lost, it simply moves from one place to another. The thing with energy in our lives is that we could mistake this energy principle for the idea of fairness. For some reason, we think that life should be fair, or that there should be a 'give and take' relationship with the world around us, and that concept lets us down big time.

Here are a few good examples.

- Karma. When you do good or bad things, good or bad things will return to you respectively.
- The ancient proverb 'As ye give, so shall ye receive.' (When we do good to others, good things should come back to us.)
- When we work hard we expect to be rewarded financially. Fair trade.
- When we fall in love with somebody we instinctively feel they should love us in return.

But ideas such as 'give and ye shall receive' or 'the law of karma' do not always seem to apply during our life on earth. Bad things happen to good people and vice versa. We work hard and then lose our job. We love somebody and they reject us. As life goes on, we feel more and more disappointed and disillusioned with the world.

You will have noticed that often things are very unfair. You do good things, work hard, are nice to people, etc., and yet this is not always returned. We end up getting hurt, ripped off, disappointed and let down by others. Ultimately we end up experiencing loss, feeling exhausted, depressed, sad, sick, and grieving. These examples show how these energy equilibrium concepts actually fail us.

Remember the first law of physics? It states that energy simply moves from one place to another, and this happens without a conscience. Nowhere do we see that energy must return to where it came from in equal share. There is zero happiness to be found looking at the world around us for recognition or equity. These 'fairness' ideas are actually false concepts, as this world is not fair at all, and the sooner we accept that, the better.

Energy exchange in the sense of fairness and balance is an entirely false concept, as energy on the level of this lower physical, material world simply moves from one form to another and it has no real destiny, higher intelligence, or kind intent behind it. It simply follows the basic laws of physics. Many people are living on this purely physical level and operate emotionally in the same fashion, just like animals. We can't expect higher laws to apply here. For the sake of this exercise, we will term this worldly energy experience the 'horizontal energy exchange'.

The nature of this horizontal energy exchange with the world around us leads us to become stressed, angry, and eventually sick. This temporary physical world will never bring us true lasting happiness and peace. It's all a mirage or an illusion. True lasting happiness can only be found by connecting with the higher source of infinite, unconditional healing energy from above. Similar to how plants receive light from the sun, we need to turn our inner being upwards to receive healing light in the form of soft, comforting, peaceful energy.

This is a vertically moving energy and it comes down on us from a higher realm. The only thing we need to do to receive this endless reservoir of energy is to tune in and resonate with it, which we will talk about more in chapter 4.

An analogy I often use for the source of unconditional healing energy is our sun. There are some striking similarities. For example, the sun appears to have infinite energy, and it asks for nothing in return. In fact, if you tried to give the sun something it would simply burn it up before it got close. Even the entire earth would vaporise if it got close enough.

When you feel the sun on your body, it has this incredibly warm glowing feeling, like a comforting healing effect. Healing energy also has this warm, comforting nature, and we will talk more about this later. So, how can we use this vertical energy concept for healing? Consider these key principles.

- The source of healing energy is universal, infinite and unconditional.
- It supplies a one-way endlessly flowing energy and requires nothing in return.
- Energy moves 'impartially' from one place or state to another place or state.
- As our capacity to receive energy from above then release and channel healing energy outward increases, healing will take place within us.
- As a result, the old pattern of needing to obtain energy from the world around us decreases, and happiness increases.

- The only thing potentially standing in the way is our ego, with its limited worldly beliefs, attitudes or opinions.

You can see roughly how this energy exchange might look in the diagram opposite.

Healing energy flow explained

The phrase 'As ye give, so shall ye receive' is only true when you understand that what you will receive when giving energy only comes from above, and only flows when we resonate with the source above, and the channel is opened. It is entirely futile to expect healing energy to come from the world around you. It is primarily our beliefs, opinions and attitudes (our ego stuff) that expect this, actually blocking energy flow, bringing disappointment, causing pressure and stress, and eventually making us sick. Just to clarify, I'm not talking about absolute knowledge or truth, which is in harmony with the healing energy source. The ego stuff I'm referring to is our own constructed self-serving stuff, and our so-called baggage.

Our physical body is the direct result of these mental attitudes and their emotional consequences. Because up to 90 per cent of our opinions, beliefs and attitudes are fear-based and typically don't align with absolute truth — they just get in the way, blocking the flow of healing energy. Central to this entire picture is the false expectation of energy returning from the world around us, equally and fairly.

Again, because this goes against the universal law of physics in terms of energy flow, it causes us to feel disappointed, tired, hungry, heavy, under pressure, angry, sad and frustrated within, thus causing stress, grief and pain, both physical and emotional. Eventually, this results in the disease process.

Trying to retain energy for ourselves is the biggest mistake we make, and this type of energy retention will make us unwell, a bit like energy

Infinite Energy Reservoir
Ego Must Go
NEW One-way
Vertical Energy
NEW One-way
Vertical Energy
OLD Two-way
Horizontal Energy
OLD Two-way
Horizontal Energy

constipation. Our oldest beliefs, attitudes and opinions hold back the majority of this energy, which builds up, increasing pain and pressure within us.

When we focus on completely dropping our ego or allowing ourselves to simply experience things as they really, truly are, we let go, and we make space, thus removing the clouds of resistance, and allowing healing energy to flow.

This generally requires a humbling shift in our core philosophy on life, and that is when we receive actual knowledge, truth, light and healing. Humility is the key. Nothing is lost, it simply moves on, and changes form. We then have access to the healing power that comes from above, causing any stored and trapped energy to melt away.

Our ego will say, 'I know all I need to know', but we must ignore that loud voice of rebellion, pride and contempt, and listen to the gentle whisper of our heart. Beliefs can then be replaced by knowledge and pain transformed into bliss. Healing energy can be felt flowing through our heart and mind, and healing takes place.

The more we drop our ego and let go, the more we receive, because the source is infinite.

Remember the law of conservation, 'energy simply moves' — and if it's healing energy then it's infinite and unconditional. All you need to do is stop looking to the world around you for energy and start looking for energy from above. Think vertical, and let it go.

Now you're prepared to start tuning in to the healing energy.

My story continues . . .

As a lad, 10–14 years old, I remember having many discussions with my family about the mysterious, the mystical and the unknown. I was truly fascinated by these subjects. My favourite book was an encyclopaedia-type book entitled *The Universe*. I could read it over and over and never tire of the wonder of the beauty and scale of our universe. I would ask my father and my grandparents around the dinner table for their views. Did the universe have a beginning or an end? When did it start and when will it finish? I was certain there was such a thing as infinity and I wanted to somehow grasp the concept with my mind. I also heard many stories from my father about his childhood with a spiritualist dad. I never met this grandad, as he

died before I was born, but I was ever intrigued by the stories of the spiritual encounters my father had. He talked of furniture levitating in the air, voices coming out of floating objects and the house shaking with tremors during their gatherings. I also had other members of my own family talk about these and other things in a very matter-of-fact fashion. This made me very accepting of the possibility of other dimensions and the existence of intelligences beyond this realm. You don't necessarily need to have this belief to access healing energy, but I'm sure it's helped me keep the walls down, and stay open to having an ability to work in the healing arts. We will pick my story up again at the end of each chapter.

Chapter 3:

What is healing energy?

We have previously discussed placing ourselves in the right headspace to connect with healing energy, and described the unconditional nature of healing energy, and in the next chapter we'll talk about resonating and tuning in. But first what exactly is this healing energy?

In order to heal, our body needs to clearly receive and respond to the complete informational blueprint that our DNA has programmed into it. We now know that our DNA not only carries our parental genetic code, but also responds to environmental factors, and throughout our lifetime genes can switch on and off. Active genes can be switched off, and inactive genes that may not be functioning correctly can be switched on. This has given rise to an increasing field of research called epigenetics. This has clearly revealed the fact that environmental influences can powerfully affect our genes.[1]

Electromagnetic energy

The fact that we receive information from our environment in the form of electromagnetic (EM) energy is a critical point to understanding what healing energy is. For example, we see light and we feel heat, which are both variable forms of EM energy.

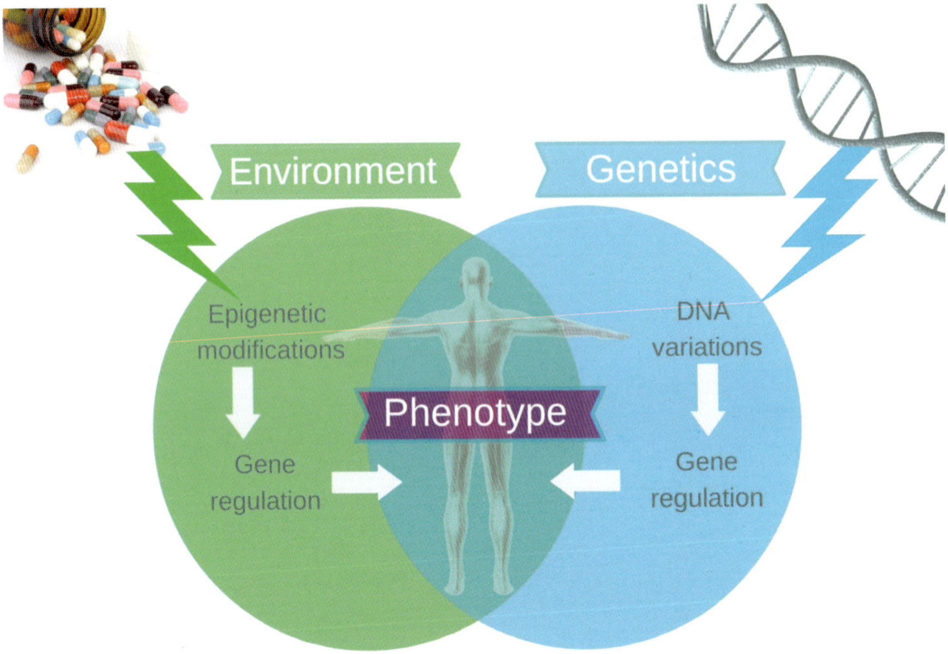

We also use electromagnetic energy in the form of radio, microwave (satellites, phones) and digital (fibre-optics) to communicate information with our technology. Because healing energy also has this electromagnetic quality, it's worth discussing these similitudes.

As we discussed in the previous chapter, a great analogy for the source of healing energy is the sun. We know that life on this planet relies on energy from the sun. Plants capture the EM energy from the sun, then use photosynthesis to store this energy (chlorophyll), which is transformed into plant sugars (carbohydrates) to feed our metabolism. And as we discussed, we don't need to give anything to the sun, yet it freely gives out life energy.

Another similarity between the sun and healing energy is the way it behaves. For example, when clouds appear or we walk into the shadows, the energy appears to fade and diminish. At night the earth falls into darkness, but the sun itself continues to shine. You could say the same thing applies to healing energy. When clouds appear in our lives, or our minds become disturbed with the complexities of life, healing energy appears to decrease and we feel weak, empty and tired. The fact is, however, that the healing energy has never stopped shining upon us, we simply needed to step out of the shadows, clear our minds, and instantly the sun shines upon us again.

The most striking parallel between sunlight and healing energy is in its electromagnetic character. So let's have a look at this amazing spectrum of electromagnetism, or as I like to call it, the spectrum of light. After all, electromagnetism is just various forms of light energy.

In order to expand on this a little, let's discuss our world in terms of this EM energy. I won't go into any in-depth science or physics but I would like to examine the potentials we have at our fingertips regarding energy, and what we can do with it to heal ourselves.

Most of us are familiar with the spectrum of visible light, as we've all seen a rainbow. We know that plants trap this light energy, which becomes the metabolic energy source for all living things. Hence, we get light energy indirectly from the sun in our food. But what about all the other EM energy that is around us and within us, and what exists beyond the spectrum of visible light?

Have a quick look at the diagram of the EM light spectrum on the following page. This is the spectrum of EM energy. More than 99.99 per cent of this spectrum is unseen by the human eye, but a great percentage of it can be subtly felt, by our own personal energy field.

You can see on the chart how the tiny visible light fraction fits into the grand scheme of things. It plays a very small part. On either side of visible light are other EM waves of varying length that also transmit energy and are sometimes used to transmit extremely condensed information. By the way, the jury is out regarding light as energy or particles, or both. It behaves as if it were both, so let's allow for this possibility. In other words, when we receive light or healing energy, we may actually be receiving subtle matter of some kind.

At the wide end, we have radio waves. They transmit a tremendous amount of complex information through our atmosphere and also through space. Thanks to microwave satellites we also enjoy high-definition television pictures with surround sound, all travelling around the world instantly. The EM spectrum extends beyond this diagram in both directions, but how far we don't really know. This means that we have, built into our planet and our universe, an incredibly powerful information highway with virtually infinite potential.

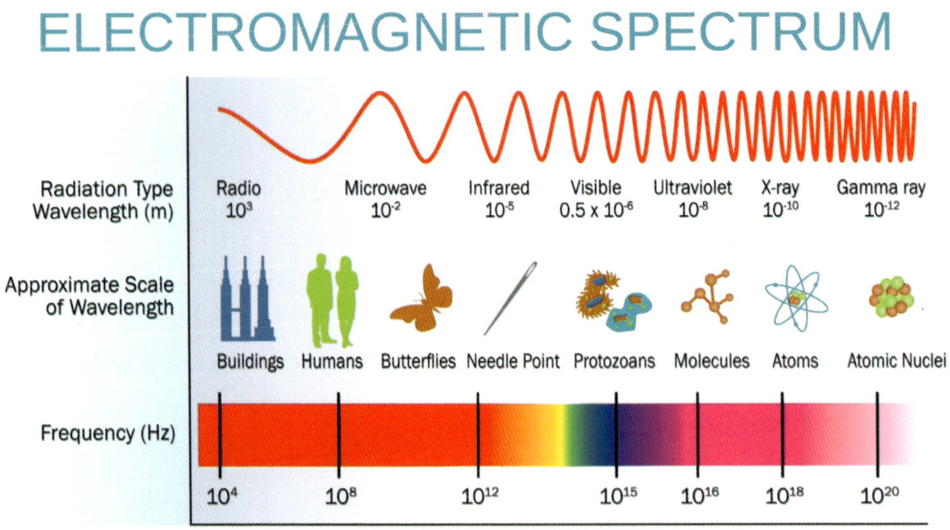

At the narrow end of the spectrum, you have gamma radiation, which is emitted by the sun. This energy is powerful enough to penetrate our planet directly through its core. This means that even at night while you are sleeping, gamma rays from the sun are passing through your body continuously.

What I find intriguing about this spectrum is its infinite potential for energy and information transmission. If you consider the amount of information transferred by television satellites at the low-frequency end of the spectrum, then how much more can be sent at the high-frequency end? If you compare the wavelengths then the difference is clear.

Radio waves can be the length of a football field or longer, and gamma rays can be smaller than the nucleus of an atom. The shorter the wave, the higher the frequency, and the more information can potentially be carried in a shorter timeframe, but the longer waves are more powerful over a longer distance, so there is merit in both the high and low frequencies.

A great example of this capacity is the microwave satellite technology that we already use for communications and television. In fact, the entire universe has a continuous, uniform, warm, cosmic microwave background (CMB), and I suspect this could indicate the location of our infinite healing energy reservoir.[2] We will talk more about tapping into this reservoir later.

Because we understand less than 10 per cent of our universe, frequencies beyond the scope of our current scientific discoveries must exist, and this is where healing energy lies waiting, still to be found by science. This gives rise to the possibilities of universal, cosmic and spiritual energies that may be miles off our charts. If you consider that the spark of life, human consciousness, love and emotions are also off the science charts, there appears to be an obvious connection.

Cosmic plasma

Traditionally we are taught about matter as being in three states — solid, liquid or gas — and the fourth state, plasma, is not mentioned. This universal, cosmic plasma is actually the fourth state of matter and is found everywhere in the universe, making up perhaps 99 per cent of our universe. Plasmas pervade intergalactic space, interstellar space, interplanetary space and the space environments of the planets. This plasma is interwoven within the electromagnetic fields throughout the universe, and the nature of their interactions is as yet unclear to scientists. In other words, we have a finer form of matter than the gasses, and this largely 'invisible matter' is intrinsically connected with the EM fields of light and, potentially, information.

Over the last decade, 'plasma medicine' has become a booming interdisciplinary research topic of growing importance that explores enormous opportunities at the interface of chemistry, plasma physics and the biomedical sciences.[3]

This poses a few questions. Are these universal EM fields responsible for carrying the information behind the structure, formation and behaviour of our physical universe? Is there information quietly hidden within subtle EM frequencies that give rise to organised matter and life by transfer of intelligent design data, thus influencing cosmic plasma? I know, these are deep questions. But again I emphasise the limitations of current science, which understands less than 1 per cent of everything there is to know, hence the possibilities of infinite healing energy remain wide open.

If we spent the same amount of time and money investigating human energy fields, consciousness, and the direct transfer of intelligence through plasma as we do sending probes into space, I'm sure we'd be all the more enlightened as a species by now.

There are some striking parallels between our modern scientific methods of communicating and healing with EM energy, and the traditional concept of a great universal consciousness that communicates and heals. Seeing these two disciplines side-by-side shows how science and religion are likely both accessing the same field of EM energy, albeit on various frequencies.

- **Science** — In global communication networks, the EM energy field is used to send information across vast distances, and in the medical arena, it's used in both diagnostic and therapeutic interventions. This includes X-ray, MRI and CT scans, radiotherapy, plasma and laser treatment, to mention just a few.[4]
- **Religion** — In many religions, God is viewed as an all-powerful (omnipotent) spiritual being, who is the holder and giver of all knowledge (omniscient), present as a great consciousness throughout the entire cosmos (omnipresent). This divine creator is also said to infuse those humans who seek a connection with

> a healing light, communicate a higher knowledge and healing throughout the entire universe.[5]

According to modern astrophysics, the invisible dark matter and dark energy in our universe is over 95 per cent* of the known cosmos and is suspected to hold together the fabric of creation from which our entire universe emerges, including the unified EM fields, and cosmic plasma.

Thousands of years ago when religions were formed and people spoke of spirits and healing powers, nobody had the faintest idea about EM or plasma and how these layers of creation could be used as healing tools, transferring energy and information. Yet all of these modern scientific discoveries fit perfectly within the scope of these spiritual traditions. You would think that if these ancient practices and beliefs were nothing but mythology and fairy tales then modern science would have found contradictions within the make-up of our universe. The opposite has unfolded. Science is inadvertently pointing to the fact that spirituality, healing and other dimensions of existence do look like definite, tangible realities.

If more than 95 per cent of the energy in our cosmos still lies outside of scientific knowledge, including things such as human consciousness, spirituality and the source of life, then it's a distinct plausible possibility that these all reside within the same realm, i.e. the realm of a great field of uncharted electromagnetic energy and plasma. In fact, I know for certain that there is such a connection, and this is where healing energy can be found.

**Authors note: Throughout this book I will refer to various 'energy' portions of our universe using various percentages. Because there are many different parts to this energy spectrum, I realise it can be confusing. There are EM waves, plasma, dark energy, dark matter, subatomic space and more, so please don't stress about the exact percentages, because even science itself does not fully understand or define these exactly. The emphasis is really on just how much of our reality is purely energy.*

You can also know this for certain by conducting the personal experiments that I'm going to share with you in this book. You can be like the scientist researching a new theory, gathering the results to draw your conclusion. The test methods you can use will be covered in the pages to come.

Prepare to go where you have not been before, allowing yourself new experiences of being connected to yourself and to the cosmos at wonderful, dizzying heights. Nothing but goodness and healing is to be found within these experiments, and this will become your testimony of the effectiveness of Unconditional Energy Healing. Let's talk about what you might feel.

How does healing energy feel?

A wonderful experience that confirms when you have made the connection to healing energy is the feeling that the energy itself brings, which may include some of the sensations below.

- **Heat or warmth** — As healing energy passes through us, just like microwaves, it breaks up complex material into simpler free energy, and as this resistance is encountered, broken down and liberated, we feel warmth or heat. It can feel like gentle sunlight on your head, back and shoulders or within your chest and core. It can also feel like a warm, golden, honey-like liquid moving slowly and taking away pain and stress from wherever it is felt.
- **Peace and comfort** — Similar to being with a loved family

member or spouse during a happy time, the warm fuzzies, or a deep sense of contentment, belonging and connectedness can occur. This is because healing energy is essentially the energy of love and represents your true nature and your eternal home.

- **Energy and lightness** — This is a feeling of incredible vitality and clarity that can make you feel light and energised, almost like you could float. Because healing energy releases heavy toxins and stress, it lifts and simplifies your molecular structure, and allows electricity to move freely throughout your body.

Everybody feels healing energy differently. Sometimes there is temporary buzzing, tingling, pressure or even pain, but this should all pass quickly, as this usually occurs when there has been a severe blockage or stress build-up of some kind.

Let's summarise

- Electromagnetic microwaves and plasma exist throughout our universe and are capable of unimaginable quantities of information transmission.
- Our cells can receive information from our environment as electromagnetic energy, which can affect our genetic expression and therefore healthy cell regeneration.
- We already use electromagnetic and plasma energy in our health system for various diagnostic and treatment methods.
- Healing energy brings warmth, light, information and life to all it touches, but most of all a deep sense of peace and love.

By now you must be starting to see that we're not talking about some 'airy-fairy' concept, but instead something real and tangible, and well within the boundaries of existing scientific understanding. Making healing energy something you can see and experience as real and attainable for you is my ultimate goal.

Think about it for a second. Just because our scientific instruments are not capable of measuring and quantifying human consciousness, such as thoughts, dreams, emotion, and feelings of love, does not mean we can't experience them ourselves. It's exactly the same with healing energy since it clearly falls into the same category.

We all know that our consciousness affects our physical body and that this can be felt. Healing energy is like the glue that holds all of these levels of our consciousness together, and it's this same glue that holds the universe together. The infinite universal energy of consciousness/electromagnetic plasma makes up this glue, and it's an integral part of who we are as energy beings.

This loving, creative information source that emits life force, knowledge, light energy and love is right there within us, waiting to be found by every soul on earth. The source shares this infinite, unconditional healing energy with us. When we connect with it we will feel an unmistakable sense of deep peace and safety, like we have found home. Then we know we have connected with healing energy.

The universal energy fields of magnetism and gravity within which the entire universe is hung and balanced are connected by this same creative power. Nothing escapes its reach and yet the flow of this energy can be impeded. We do this unintentionally by our very nature, and yet the healing energy is never far from us. It's similar to the sensor light that turns off automatically whenever we leave the room. The room may be full of truth and light, and the moment we choose to ignore or think otherwise, let our ego step in, listen to the lies of the world, or follow our self preservation-oriented 'animal nature', we step

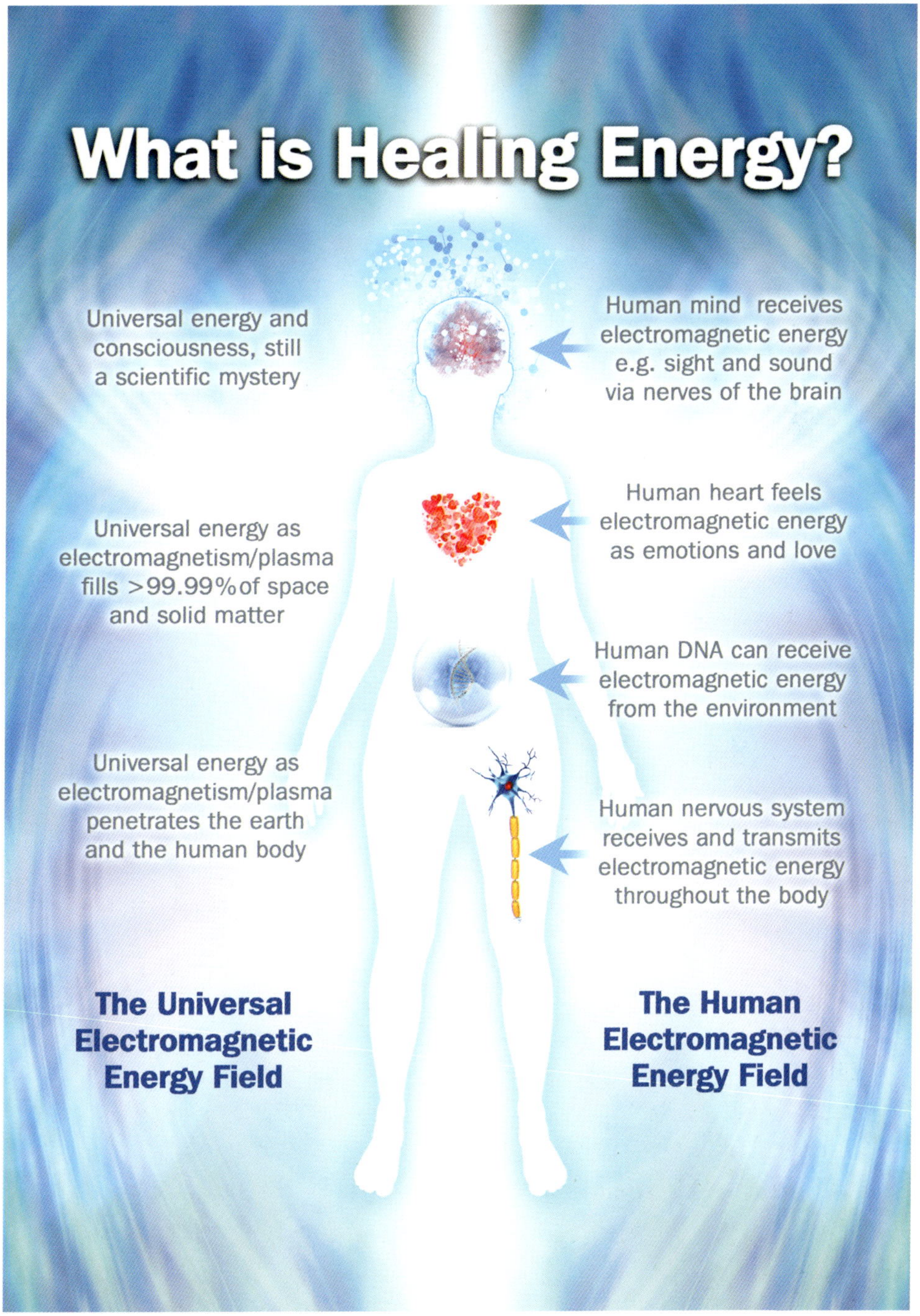
What is Healing Energy?
Universal energy and consciousness, still a scientific mystery
Human mind receives electromagnetic energy e.g. sight and sound via nerves of the brain
Universal energy as electromagnetism/plasma fills >99.99% of space and solid matter
Human heart feels electromagnetic energy as emotions and love
Human DNA can receive electromagnetic energy from the environment
Universal energy as electromagnetism/plasma penetrates the earth and the human body
Human nervous system receives and transmits electromagnetic energy throughout the body
The Universal Electromagnetic Energy Field
The Human Electromagnetic Energy Field

out of the room, and the lights switch off.

I know this is a lot to take on board, but it will all fall into place as we move on with the practical method and its applications. We've done a lot of groundwork up to this point, and the reason I've taken some time to give this much background information is that all these pieces will make the picture that much clearer, as more layers are added.

After discussing how we can tune in to this energy in chapter 4, in chapter 5 I will talk about making a clear and strong connection with healing energy and a simple technique for achieving that.

My story continues . . .

In my school years I remember feeling compassion towards the kids who were different. They may have had disabilities, were struggling with learning, or in one way or another ended up sitting on their own with no friends. I would always go and talk with them to help them feel that somebody liked them, so that they could talk about themselves. This gave me a wonderful feeling and I can only imagine they would have felt it too. Even in my early working life I was in the habit of befriending the people who seemed to be struggling to fit in. I would see them change and come out of their shell. I felt my desire to help people grow in my late teens and early twenties. At the same time I was struggling myself with addictive behaviours, smoking and drinking heavily. I was overly sensitive to my emotions, found it hard to achieve happiness in my relationships, and tended to get a broken heart very easily. All of these things I would later realise were because of my awareness and sensitivity to the healing energy, along with a very strong sense of wanting to stay connected. I think we all go through these phases of emotional pain, addiction, mental stress, heartbreak and disappointment before we begin to find our way. Sometimes it was unbearable and yet I knew there was light at the end of the tunnel. I would discover my true nature and calling if I just kept moving forward and searching.

One day in my early twenties my other grandfather handed me a book called *Supernature* by the author Lyall Watson. This book was written in 1971 and talked about bridging the gap between science and the supernatural. The most memorable part for me was when he talked about super-consciousness and collective consciousness in the animal kingdom. In one experiment termites were able to build a perfect mound on either side of a solid steel plate and make the mound summit at exactly the same point on either side. It was concluded that the termites were somehow able to communicate through the thick steel plate. Watson went on to talk about how schools of fish and flocks of birds fly together as one collective being, and related this to the human race, and how we are also connected by a collective consciousness. This really made me start to think about the power of our thoughts, and what this energy really is that connects living things. After reading this book I was inspired to start reading again, something I hadn't done since leaving school. I wanted to learn more, and that has stayed with me to this day. Learning is such a wonderful way to expand your consciousness.

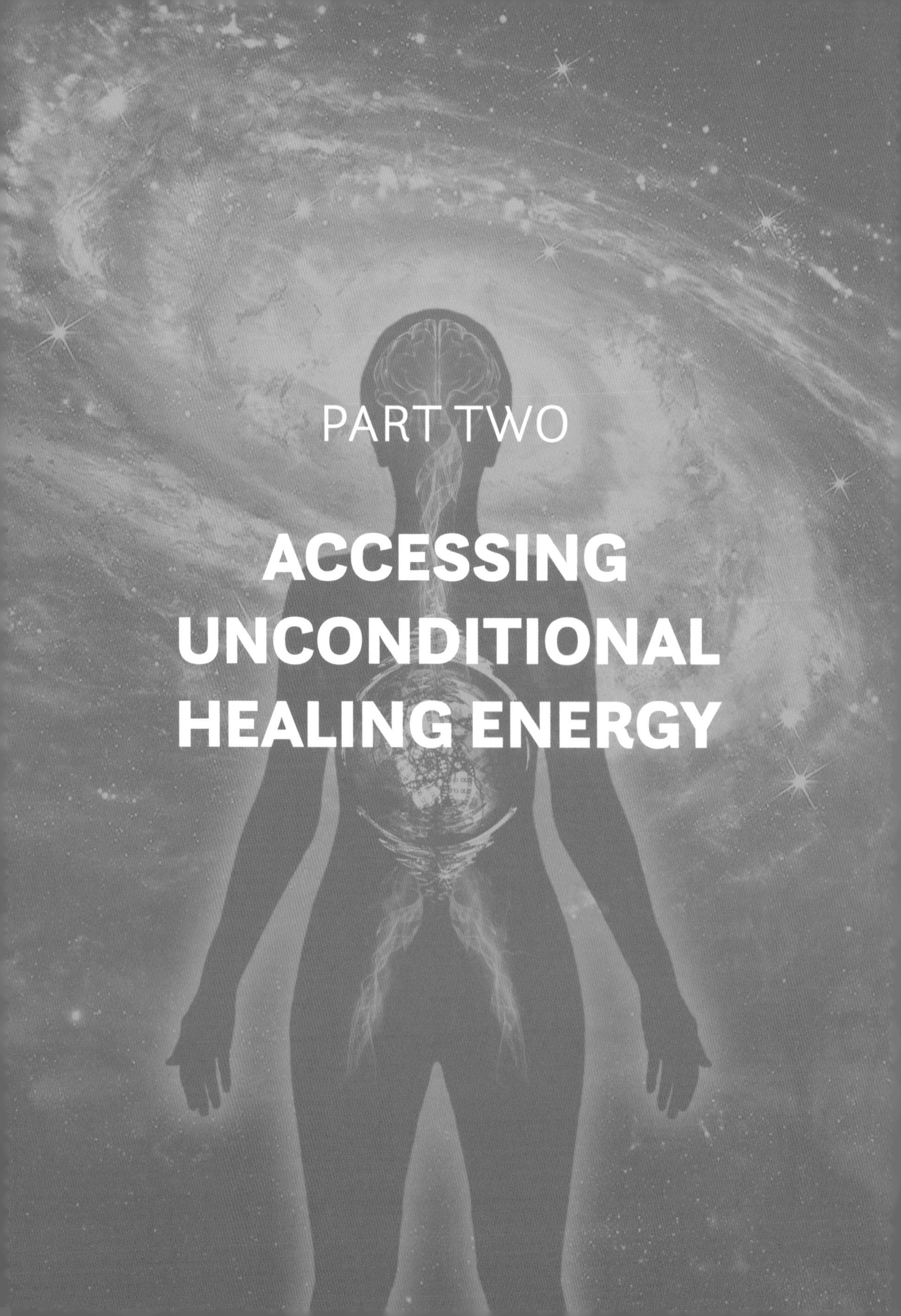

PART TWO

ACCESSING UNCONDITIONAL HEALING ENERGY

Chapter 4:

Tuning in

Healing energy is just like any other form of energy, it follows the same laws of physics, and it acts, behaves, moves and travels from one place to another in exactly the same way. In order to put ourselves in the right place to receive healing energy, we will compare other types of energy and how they are received.

A great example is mobile telephones and Sky television, which receive energy in the form of microwaves from transmitting towers and satellites in space. Radio antennae also operate using this principle. All of these various waves are forms of electromagnetic wave/particle technology. We will look at electromagnetism in more detail soon. The point here is this:

All we need to do is attune ourselves to the unconditional healing energy channel (or frequency) and we can receive a signal in the form of electromagnetic energy, which is a pulsating particle/waveform capable of carrying both energy and information.

When two devices or objects have the same tuning or frequency they resonate with each other and can communicate. The great thing about receiving energy by 'resonance' is that while one end is transmitting the other end can receive 'passively'. This means no effort or action is required by the receiver. Just like when you look at the sunset, your eyes simply receive the beautiful orange light of the setting sun without any effort on your part. That's because your eyes are already attuned to the frequency of the visible light spectrum.

This exact same principle applies when tuning in to healing energy. We only need to understand what the frequency is to tune in to this energy. As there is an infinite reservoir of healing energy available, once tuned in, we can receive an endless, infinite flow of this energy.

Because we are continuously distracted by the world around us we tend to tune in to things that are around us, which are usually disconnected from healing energy. Healing energy is hard to find in the mostly man-made physical world around us, apart from a small fraction that is available by connecting with nature. This is because pure healing energy originates from above, on the vertical axis. Remember how we talked about obtaining the highest perspective in order to connect with healing energy? The same rule applies when tuning in. We need to turn our receptive senses upwards to the higher realm of universal consciousness, which is above and beyond the world around us, and ultimately resonates with infinite unconditional love.

In a well-known physics experiment, two tuning forks of the same note are placed on a table several feet apart. One fork is struck with a hammer and makes a loud gong sound. Within moments the second tuning fork starts to make the same sound without being struck at all. This is the principle of resonance in action. If another tuning fork of differing frequency was in the vicinity of the first one being struck then it would sit dead, and make no sound. You can only resonate when attuned to the same wavelength as the source. This is exactly how the principle of 'tuning in' to healing energy operates. Once you are on the correct wavelength/frequency, you will receive healing energy without

Second tuning fork resonates by itself, but only when it's the same frequency
First tuning fork is struck
Other tuning forks tuned to different frequencies will not resonate
Resonance in Action

any effort involved. You act like the second 'passive' tuning fork, and you simply resonate with universal healing energy.

Please remember the word EFFORTLESS. This is crucial to understanding Unconditional Energy Healing. We do nothing, other than drop our ego (our past ideas), tune in and allow ourselves to resonate with the source of healing energy.

A common mistake a lot of so-called energy healers make is that they make an effort, and try to use their own energy in some way, shape or form. They try to push, manipulate or force energy using their willpower or mind. That's an entirely incorrect practice, as the healing energy is not ours, and does not belong to us. It's a bit like air: we breathe it in and we breathe it out, but it never belongs to us. If you try and use your own energy to heal, then you can drain yourself, end up feeling exhausted and you may inadvertently pick up complex stress energy from other people as a result.

A good exercise to practise tuning in is to listen. Simply sit still and listen to what's going on around you and see if you can tune in to various things. Listening intently to music is quite a good warm-up for this exercise. You can also practise tuning in to and feeling various frequencies, by being mindful, meditating and just taking time out to be still. I will expand on this method later on.

For now, I want you to consider this. When you focus on, think about, accept or believe certain things, you are essentially tuning in to certain frequencies. That which you think about and focus on generates a pattern within you and that pattern can be one of purity, peace and health, or one of disruption and stress.

It's often said that we tend to hang out with like-minded people, and that 'birds of a feather stick together'. This is perfectly natural, because we don't like to be around things or people that conflict with our personal energy. You will feel comfortable with things that are on the same wavelength or frequency as yourself. This is all very well, but if it's healing you need then it's important to look carefully at your situation, and consider if there's anything or anyone that's potentially worth disconnecting yourself from.

Without being aware of it you can be tuning in to negative people, toxic energy, and even energy parasites. This can all drag you down and leave you feeling depleted. It is important to be discerning and not allow yourself to tune in to anything that is not contributing to your higher purpose. We must be like water off a duck's back and not allow ourselves to get dragged in to others' negativity or dilemmas.

We can still show compassion, empathy, understanding and sometimes offer direct advice or help to others, but we must not 'buy in' to the drama and allow ourselves to become entangled. This can be tricky, especially when it's your immediate family, but sometimes we just have to say no. Sometimes others must learn by their own mistakes and their consequences. Maintaining a position of love and peace amongst it all is something you will learn from practising Unconditional Energy Healing within yourself.

We are all here to learn about integrating our pure unconditional loving spirit with our physical body and we can only do this when we are centred with healing energy.

Tuning in to the absolute highest source of universal energy and love is needed to bring about healing and this can be achieved simply by understanding the principle of resonance. If you want to receive healing energy you must resonate with it, and that's all there is to it. It sounds too easy, and that in itself can actually stand in your way. We spend most of our time attempting to resonate with the world around us and trying to tune in to what is mostly just entertainment and distracting interference. Because of this we expect things to be complicated, we forget the simple truth, and most of the time the healing signals fade out.

With regular practice, we can stay attuned, and when we obtain direct alignment with the absolute highest universal truths in our hearts and minds we begin to resonate with the unconditional healing energy. It's not that we generate the energy; we simply tune in to it and immediately we begin to receive its healing power.

We will talk more about this principle in the next chapter, but keep this in mind for now:

All we need to do is tune in to the source of healing energy in order to freely receive an infinite supply.

My story continues . . .

After reading my first educational material in seven years since leaving school, my mind was reawakened and I felt a glowing sense of wonder once again. There was so much more to life than I had considered before. They say knowledge is power, and that's exactly how it felt. There was a sense of energy and power coming into my mind and body as I read. This sparked a new chapter of exploration, and I started reading every book I could find on the mystic arts, philosophy, religion, meditation and self-healing. As my mind was opening to these concepts I began to directly experience energy and had some interesting visions. One thing I started seeing was large balls of light in my periphery and what looked like shafts of light radiating from above people's heads, especially outdoors. I also began to see bright blue colours around people, and sometimes swirling energy fields on the ceiling above my bed. Of course this all seemed very weird to anybody I told, so I largely kept it to myself. I did visit a psychologist once, just to check on my sanity, but he said that normal, healthy people do see these things from time to time. At the age of 23 I asked my Aunty Marie, who I knew was a spiritualist, to come over for a visit, so I could ask her about what I was seeing. She simply said 'you're

seeing energy fields', which seemed quite logical. She also asked me to put out my hand, palm up. She placed her palm down on mine and proceeded to intentionally give me an electric shock. My instinct was to shock her back, which I somehow knew how to do, by default. She jumped and exclaimed, 'Brett, you're a healer.' That was my confirmation that I had to follow a new path in life. My personal study had led me into practising meditation and I was on my way to further discoveries and experiences of healing energy from that point on.

Chapter 5:

Connecting

In the last few chapters, we've talked about getting ourselves into the 'healing energy' headspace by taking a higher perspective, understanding energy exchange, and tuning in to and resonating with the healing energy; and we have explored the nature of the energy itself.

Now we have the background information, it's time to put these things together and make real tangible connections, so you can start to experience increased levels of this healing energy for yourself, and feel it growing within you.

Our bodies actually run on electromagnetic energy and our body holds a charge just like a battery. For example, our brain, heart and nervous system are all electrical and magnetic in nature, which is why modern medicine uses so many electromagnetic devices and equipment, both in diagnosis and treatment. These include EEG and ECG scans for the brain and heart respectively, X-rays, CT scans, infrared thermography, MRI, laser, plasma technology and many more. Even the energy in our food was originally captured EM plasma energy from the sun, which is eventually liberated within the cells of our body as the spark of metabolic life released when simple sugar (glucose) and fat (glycerol) are further split apart and combusted, triggering the synthesis of other energy transport molecules.

We also receive, sense and feel energy from the world around us in a subtle, yet silently powerful EM way. Similarly, our emotions, thoughts and inner body impulses, which are largely subconscious and beyond our ability to control, also represent EM energy. In fact, this energy often influences and dictates our behaviour without our knowledge. These EM impulses (feelings) come at us from multiple sources in all directions. Without experience and training, it can become overwhelming, stressful and very confusing.

This means, in order to make the connection with healing energy strong, we will need to take more conscious control of ourselves, our emotions and our minds. This conscious control can produce a more reliable connection. I will now explain how we can do this by using a very simple principle for connecting. As always, this comes down to a universal, scientific law. I call this the 'switch' principle because the effect is similar to switching on a light bulb.

Let me explain. You will probably be familiar with the way a common electrical switch works to connect the electricity to a device and allow the energy to flow through a circuit. The flow of healing energy to our physical body works in a very similar manner.

For example, when things are going well and everything is working out in our favour, we feel positive, energised and switched on. A classic example of this switch principle is found in kinesiology, a common practice in natural medicine or natural healing circles. This involves testing a muscle while connecting with the patient with both hands, and subconsciously asking a series of health questions or testing food and medicinal substances for the muscle's reaction. Whether the muscle goes weak or gets stronger when tested indicates whether that substance is good or bad for the patient.

In other words, a simple electrical switch is taking place within the person in response to the energetic suggestion of, or proximity to, a certain substance or event. This is an inherent or instinctive switching response and can be very effective in guiding our decisions.

Let's look at an everyday example of this. When you think about going on a holiday to a resort, your energy can instantly increase as the electrical circuits in your body have switched on. But when you think about weeding the garden or cleaning the toilet, the electrical energy in your body may decrease. That's because those thoughts turn off the switch. This is your natural response to things you like or dislike, and you subconsciously choose to switch your energy on or off.

Connecting to healing energy, however, is slightly different because it has nothing to do with your personal preference. Rather, universal 'truth or falsity' are responsible for flipping the switch. Because these truths or deceptions may be beyond your knowledge or outside the scope of your conscious awareness, they can exert powerful effects on you from behind the scenes in your subconscious.

Consider this concept. When something is true, it is a fact, it is real and it exists, but when something is false, it is a lie, it is not real and therefore it does not exist. Unfortunately, you can strongly hold onto ideas and things that don't exist. Attitudes, opinions and beliefs can all fall into this category. Believing in things that are 'not real' can have devastating consequences, and can lead to grief, loss, pain, suffering, disease and tragedy. Our clever, manipulating, self-centred ego is very good at facilitating this fabrication.

No amount of belief in something false can bring healing. It could bring temporary happiness, but eventually, that happiness crashes into emptiness and deep despair. It's a bit like the false high and delusion created by a synthetic drug. Because the high was fake, the pending reality is a painful wake-up call — hence the morning-after hangover effect. This is an important concept to grasp when it comes to healing because even temporary 'placebo' healings can take place, but they simply don't last. Real healing is a permanent step in health and progress, with no rebound effect.

You might ask, how can a belief be false? The concept that something could be true until it is proven with absolute certainty to be false, allows people to hang on to false beliefs and non-existent objects. This relies on the initial assumption that the belief is true, or the object exists, until proven otherwise.[1]

For example, we have many fantastical ideas about flying horses, mermaids, dragons and mythical gods and demons. These have been dreamed up by mankind over the millennia, and they have taken up a place in our cultures, society and reality, whether they actually exist or not. However, if you spent your entire life looking for a mermaid or a flying horse then you would feel more and more disappointed as time goes on, and would eventually feel sad, isolated, empty and lost. A lie can never lead to lasting happiness.

It's only when we understand, accept or believe something that is actually universally true, and real, that there can be a connection to the universal source of all truth, light, intelligence, and life, ultimately connecting us to that source, and allowing healing energy to flow.

On the other hand, when we accept or believe something that is false, it's not a reality, therefore, it does not actually exist. This means there's no energy connection available. Just like a light switch turning off, there is a disconnect, and energy can't flow. As a result, we feel a sense of darkness, and are left empty, sad, drained or depressed, and can become unwell. We can only connect to healing energy when we have the truth.

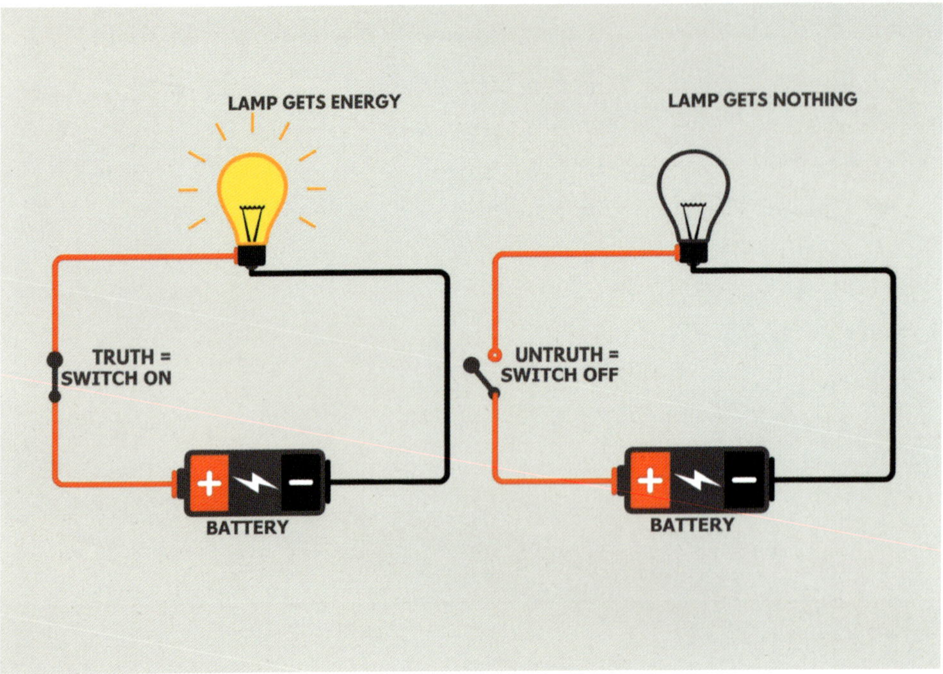

As we go through life, we are fed a multitude of lies and untruths. We are deceived, misled and ultimately start to feel disconnected. Many adults feed us false ideas when we are children. Peers can be unkind and convince us we are not good enough. The education system and even science can get things wrong. Negative experiences, loss, grief, pain and stress affect us all, but how we respond is determined by what we have been taught and what we choose to believe is true. If untrue ideas have been accepted into our world construct then our responses to life can lead us further and further into dark places.

There are literally thousands of subtle false beliefs we may have taken on, and likewise, thousands of truths we may not yet fully understand. I will share some of these shortly. You could spend many lifetimes trying to sort through them all and ultimately you may never know for sure, especially by relying on your logical mind. Using logic can also convince us to believe false and incorrect things. The ego uses logic to convince us that we are better, or worse, than other people. That's why we mentioned earlier how important it is to drop your ego, beliefs, attitudes and opinions. Good and evil are also man-made concepts to describe the difference between truth and lies. Evil is in fact simply a belief in falsity that leads to a disconnect from universal healing energy, resulting in emptiness and darkness and all that comes with it. The absolute universal truth emanates from a realm above all of these human constructs.

Healing energy is a powerful tool to bring us clarity about what is true belief, because healing energy can switch on and off just like a light bulb, and give us a clear indication of what is absolutely true and what is false. In the Bible, for example, it says, 'But the Comforter, which is the Holy Ghost, whom the Father will send in my name, he shall teach you all things, and bring all things to your remembrance' (John 14:26). You could say in the same way that the unconditional healing energy is like this 'holy spirit' that teaches us all things. When we open up and listen to the truth, it switches on, and we can feel its presence within us as peace, love and comfort, but only when we are thinking, accepting and believing that which is true. The opposing negative, dark, heavy feelings, therefore, represent untruth.

The only sure way to stay connected to the source of healing energy is with absolute unshakeable universal truths. This understanding is something that can overcome virtually all obstacles in life and bring a secure, strong connection to healing power, along with clear, reliable intuition. The more you become aware of what healing energy feels like, the more you will find clarity and guidance in your heart and mind. If you want the answer to any question in life, you can use this principle to find your answer. This is such a simple principle, from which develops a powerful technique for connecting to healing energy.

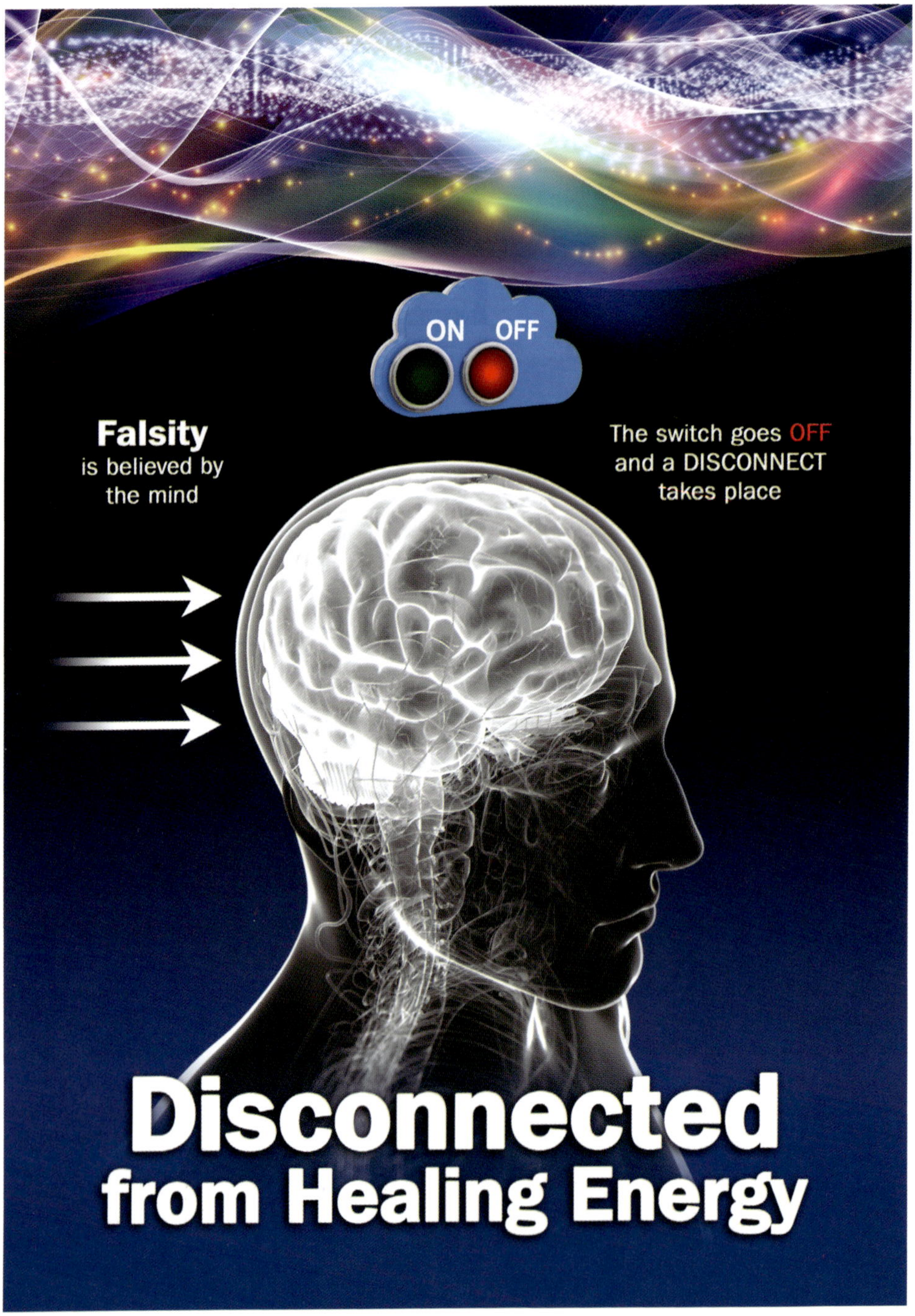
ON
OFF
Falsity
is believed by the mind
The switch goes OFF and a DISCONNECT takes place
Disconnected
from Healing Energy

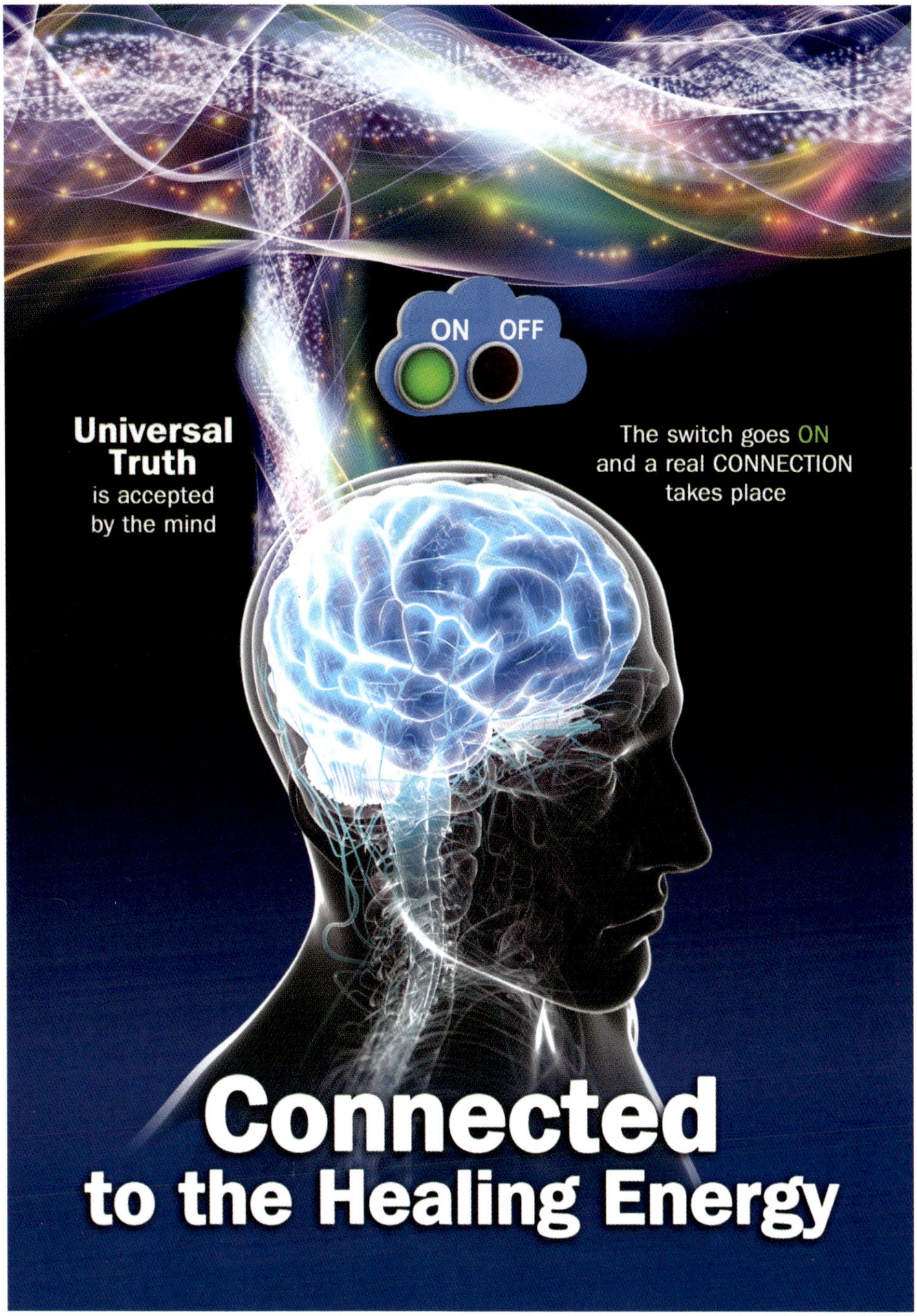
ON OFF
Universal Truth is accepted by the mind
The switch goes ON and a real CONNECTION takes place
Connected to the Healing Energy

Examples of a disconnect

Example 1: I'm not good enough

Many of us go through experiences in life that cause us to feel we don't measure up. We may fail a test, be unable to participate well in sport, or may not fit in with the group dynamic. We often develop a belief that we are unworthy, have little to offer, or that we are of no value. The most common belief around this is 'I'm not good enough'. This is a classic example of a false belief and leaves us feeling disconnected and sometimes sad or depressed. The absolute truth is, you are highly valued, you are very precious, and you are one of the greatest creations in the universe, an eternal spirit being. This truth can dispel the old lie, and connect you to healing energy. You will know immediately when you accept it, by an increase in your energy within. Try thinking about this for a few minutes and see how it feels: 'I am eternal.'

Example 2: Nobody loves me

This is probably the most common untruth. We start off getting regular hugs from our mother as a baby and infant. We then head to school and encounter bullying, rejection, emotional abuse and other isolating events. As young adults we eventually find somebody we like, and perhaps fall in love with them. These early relationships often fall apart and heartbreak is inevitable. We yearn to be loved again like the baby in our mother's arms, but it's complicated as an adult. As relationship trials continue through life we can develop the belief 'I'm unworthy of love', which can make us feel very sad indeed. This couldn't be further from the truth and is a complete switch-off. Sometimes we will hit rock bottom before we turn around and realise, 'I must first learn to love myself before others can love me' and therefore 'I am worthy of love'. This moment is when many people connect with healing energy from above and have a realisation: 'I'm either going to die sad, alone and feeling sorry for myself, or I'm going to change my thinking, be positive and start working on myself and my own inner connection to this universal energy that I now feel.' An epiphany has occurred, and the switch has been flipped on. Try thinking on this for a few minutes and see how it feels: 'I am loved.'

The one absolute all-encompassing universal truth that is above all others is 'unconditional love'. In the same way that sunlight contains millions of colours, and experts estimate that we can distinguish perhaps as many as 10 million colours,[2] unconditional healing energy contains millions of subtle truths. Pure love, just like white light, contains them all. When you are experiencing true unconditional love for another human being, you are experiencing a pure connection to unconditional healing energy and absolute truth. This type of LOVE, in capital letters, represents the highest of universal laws and contains

all we need to heal our body, mind and spirit.

I'm speaking about a particular type of universal love. This is not merely a romantic love, or the love for family; or those close to us; it is a love that is above and beyond all human limitations. As we talked about earlier, we must rise above our conditioning related to culture, language, religion, nation or anything that divides us as human beings, in order to connect 100 per cent with pure universal healing energy.

We must accept, and crystallise in our minds, the fact that we are all spiritual beings living a temporary physical existence on this planet together. We are all struggling to come to terms with the limitations these clumsy physical bodies have, and the difficulties this physical existence comes with. We all stumble, falter, lose control and make mistakes, so we're all worthy of compassion, understanding and forgiveness. This must consistently be our 'higher perspective'.

It's nurturing and developing this universal view until it becomes a permanent standpoint that generates a pure genuine love for all humanity. This puts us in the highest place possible within ourselves and opens the door to absolute truth, and the highest of universal laws, the law of unconditional love.

Another common falsity goes back to the very beginning: the belief that the world is not fair because it does not return to us the energy that it should; or that because we have given much, the world owes us a favour. This leads us down a path of false expectations, entitlement, frustration, anger, misery and doubts for the future. We continually expect things from the world, and the endless disappointments leave us in a state of constant fear. If things haven't worked out in the past then they won't work out in the future. That's entirely false.

Things around us are the direct result of what we can manifest with the energy we channel. Remember the energy exchange from chapter 2? There is not an equal return from the world, but rather energy transfer and an outer manifestation of our released energy. It never was our energy, and it never will be. We are simply the channel. If you create something, then great. If you love it, then let it go. Give it away and expect nothing in return. More energy will come from the infinite source above, but it has no obligation to return to you from the physical world below. You can sell it for a dollar, but don't expect any favours from the world. If you're good at this connecting and channelling of energy, then things will have no choice but to manifest in the world around you. That's entirely your responsibility.

We become co-creators in the universe and things manifest in the world around us simply because we create these things with our released energy. That's the real secret. We start to take control of ourselves and are not so controlled by our expectations of the world around us. Ultimately, we don't get energy from the world around us, but we can gain an appreciation for the creator by observing the creation. When we look at the things that manifest in this world we can indirectly connect with the creator.

Consider this. When you observe a work of art, a fine piece of architecture or listen to a good piece of music, you feel uplifted. It's because you are affected by the effort and expertise that went into the creation. You are tuning in and connecting to the energy of the creators of those things. When you take in a beautiful sunset, or landscape vista, you may feel a connection to the intelligent universal creator. The fact that we resonate with this intelligence should remind us that we are also creators. We don't get energy from the world, but rather we channel energy into this world.

We must always keep this in mind when looking to the world for happiness. Good things around us are the result of our own energy output and nothing else. All we can do is maintain an attitude of gratitude to the infinite supplier of energy from above, and more will come by default — because it's unconditional.

There are many other absolute truths, and also many small deceptions we have possibly fallen for, and many thousands of possible points of disconnect, maybe millions. We will talk more about some of these truths and falsities in coming chapters.

The point of the 'switch' analogy is ultimately this. When we believe something that is 'absolutely true', the switch goes on, a connection takes place, and healing energy begins to flow. Healing light enters the body in the form of tangible electromagnetic energy, our DNA is better activated and remembers more of its original informational pattern, or perhaps even, its more advanced pattern. The healing process is triggered!

You may have felt more of this healing energy as you have been reading these words. This is how you can know when something is true. The energy of peace and comfort will manifest within you in ever-increasing amounts.

The next question is, how do we actually channel this energy through our bodies to heal ourselves?

My story continues . . .

After reading many books and meditating daily, gazing into the night sky, I started wondering what I should do with my life. I was talking with my mother one day about what I was going through and she said, 'I know a good healer — you should go and see her for a session', which I immediately booked. In the session Sandie got me to lie down on a massage table and she laid her hands on my head. What happened next blew my mind. It felt like I was being electrocuted, and the energy was pulsing through my body in waves, and it caused my whole body to shudder. Above me on the ceiling was an incredible display. I saw a bright ball of white light, about the size of a baseball, spinning rapidly around in circles about 60 cm in diameter. It had a tail like a small comet. This was the most clear vision of energy that I had ever seen. My eyes were open and it was the early afternoon, so this was no dream. This was yet another experience that I could not deny. I did visit a few other practitioners, including Arlette, a kinesiologist. She taught classes called 'touch for health', which sparked my interest, so I went to a few workshops and experimented with the technique. I also learned reiki from Wim, another practitioner. I was getting qualified! I then realised that I needed some further education and enrolled in both an applied science degree and a diploma in herbal studies. The subjects of biochemistry and biophysics absolutely fascinated me, as did herbal medicine. I was on a journey of discovery into both the world of personal experiences and the world of science. I think this is when the penny dropped, that I needed a foundation of knowledge on which to build myself a solid methodology if I was going to help others with healing. My studies have continued to this day. Knowledge truly is power, but only if it's absolutely correct and applied in context.

Chapter 6:

Tapping in

I've said this many times already, but it's worth repeating because it is so key to the method of Unconditional Energy Healing. The energy supply for healing is infinite and similar in nature to the energy of our sun, but on a much more universal scale. This means we have a never-ending supply of this energy, similar to a reservoir of drinking water that never runs out. It's actually the energy that our eternal spirit body feeds on. A bit like food for our physical body, except this is food for our eternal soul.

Theoretically, we can treat healing energy in exactly the same way as a reservoir that we can tap into. We always have access to this vertically oriented healing energy deep within ourselves, but in the same way as water moves through a pipe to be released, a tap must first be opened, providing space for the water (or energy, in this instance) to flow.

The issue we have as human beings is that we are so busy all the time, especially in our minds, with a wide array of things we need to be conscious of, planning for and worrying about. This crowds our heads with constant processing activity.

We've established that healing energy comes from above and moves downwards and outwards through our bodies. To start encouraging this healing energy to move through our physical body we first need to create some space for this energy to move into. All energy ultimately behaves in the same way as liquids and gasses, and will naturally move where there is space available. If you want to attract energy, the simplest thing to do is create space, and energy will automatically come. This process is often referred to as simple diffusion. Remember that what we attract to fill such a space is determined by where we direct ourselves energetically, what we have tuned in to, and if we have a secure connection.

The easiest and quickest way to create the necessary space within us is to quieten the mind and the thinking process, and the most effective way of achieving that is with a simple meditation. Over the next few pages, we're going to tap the healing energy reservoir by sharing possibly the most powerful meditation method to quieten the mind and create healing space. Now, let's intentionally attract healing energy to start moving.

The energy reservoir

According to modern astrophysics, the entire universe is <0.1 per cent solid matter and >99.9 per cent dark matter, dark energy and other 'invisible subatomic wave/energy stuff'.[1] Scientists now acknowledge that this invisible matter/energy is what mysteriously designs, creates and supports the structure of the visible universe and also continues to cause its expansion.[2] It fills what was previously thought to be nothing but empty space, i.e. outer space itself. This invisible stuff also fills the 'inner space' within the fabric of the visible material world in which we live, filling the gaps that exist inside atoms. Coincidentally, this invisible stuff that exists absolutely everywhere fits right alongside the proposed infinite nature of the spiritual realm, an omnipresent God, or other versions of the creative force, source or creator.

Interestingly, dark energy is quite mysterious, because this infinite energy does not disperse or dilute, but rather retains a constant density, even as the universe rapidly expands. This goes entirely against the basic laws of physics and defies understanding, as it should be losing its density and slowly running out of supply. The only explanation is that dark energy must be infinite and actually emanate from another dimension above and beyond that which we presently consider part of our universe. Yet, this realm continually feeds our universe with an endless stream of ultra-fine, ultra-pure raw material. Just like our universe, our very own bodies grow from within and continue to expand outwardly — and I don't just mean gaining weight! I'm talking about cellular growth and regeneration. Within a few weeks, we grow billions of new cells and can replace old or damaged tissue. Every living thing inherently grows from within and expands in exactly the same way as the universe itself. In this way, we are intrinsically connected to the universe and its creative force energetically.

Likewise, healing energy is within the fabric of our world and feeds us with information and energy to continue growing and regenerating. I refer to it as unconditional healing energy. After all, the term 'heal' means to make whole. As we gain stronger connections to this healing energy and the information that comes with it, our genetic, metabolic, cellular, mental and even our emotional signals become more intact, complete and whole. Consequently, over time, we can potentially regenerate 100 per cent correctly and be healed.

An ancient method used all around the world, which is known to open a channel and to connect us with this inner realm, is the practice of meditation. There any many different forms and various techniques that can be applied in meditation, but I'm going to give you a specific method for tapping into healing energy.

For the sake of this 'tapping in' meditation exercise, I will mainly talk about inner light and sound and briefly touch on the term 'spirit'. I will keep this uncomplicated, and generic, as I want you to keep an open mind and grab the full potential of the meditation without challenging any belief, religion or thought system. That's my rationale for keeping this all as science-based as possible.

The benefits of meditation

There is only one ultimate purpose or desired end result of any traditional meditation practice and that is 'spiritual illumination'. During meditation, we proceed to open up our senses until our 'sixth sense' is stimulated and activated. You have your own unique healing path to find and that is what this process is here to facilitate. All I have set out to do is open up a few doors and windows in your heart and mind with the desire to empower your transformation and healing. The meditations are based on this same principle, expanding your window of consciousness, so as to broaden your view, open up the inner channels and give you a direct experience of healing energy.

The benefits of meditation have been well documented and include experiences of ecstasy, peace, stress and pain relief, slowed aging, plus a reduction in many diseases.[3]

I have been meditating most of my life and have looked at a multitude of different techniques. I believe the method I have developed and that I describe in this chapter will bring you the quickest, most powerful healing results, and the quickest spiritual progress of any method in the world. Best of all, you can slot it right in with whatever knowledge, beliefs or religion you might already have.

During meditation, we may see, hear and feel things that appear to originate in another dimension. We can become partially aware of the greater than 99.9 per cent invisible fraction of our universe. This in itself can change our perspective on life. This can change how we view our world and our lives for the better, in many ways. We may find many benefits along the way, such as health, energy, clarity of mind, higher intellect, greater perception, bliss, love and many other resulting changes that can spill over into our lives, but spiritual illumination and healing are the ultimate outcomes.

By experiencing this you may realise the higher truth about who you are and what it is you should do with your life. Your body will feel the changes, emotionally and physically, very quickly. Your sense of colour and taste can become more pronounced. Peace of mind and clarity of thought can be enhanced. Intuition and guidance may start to become a little more than coincidental in your life.

It has been suggested that group meditation can affect large numbers of people for the better. Studies have shown that crime rates tend to drop when large groups meditate together.[4] This shows the power of meditation to influence and heal your surroundings. Imagine what it can do within your family, workplace and personal health.

As you connect with the higher power at work in our universe and channel that power through your mind and body as information waves, you begin to radiate this energy, directly impacting everything around you. You start to send out a signal like a transmitter and all things around you respond in some way. Peace, love, harmony, happiness, energy and light will appear to radiate from within you and affect your surroundings subtly.

Healing is a natural by-product of the type of meditation I'm about to share with you.

The meditation process

I'll share the meditation method I have found works best. It comes in three major parts, which we will call exercises, all of which are ideally combined into your meditation.

Preparation

Before you begin, find a quiet space where you can sit and be comfortable, relax and not be interrupted. You can lie down if you want, but sitting works slightly better, as you tend to stay awake longer. Falling asleep is fine, but staying awake means you will consciously remember more of the energy experience.

Close your eyes and allow yourself to breathe deeply and slowly. If you know the yoga breathing method you can employ that, but simply put: breathe deeply and slowly into your belly, breathing in through your nose and exhaling out through your mouth.

To start getting results quickly with meditation, it pays to keep it very simple.

- You will get better results by sitting upright as gravity seems to encourage a better energy flow when sitting.
- Crossed legs and clasped hands also help create an electrical circuit.
- You can also do this when lying down before going to sleep or before rising in the morning.

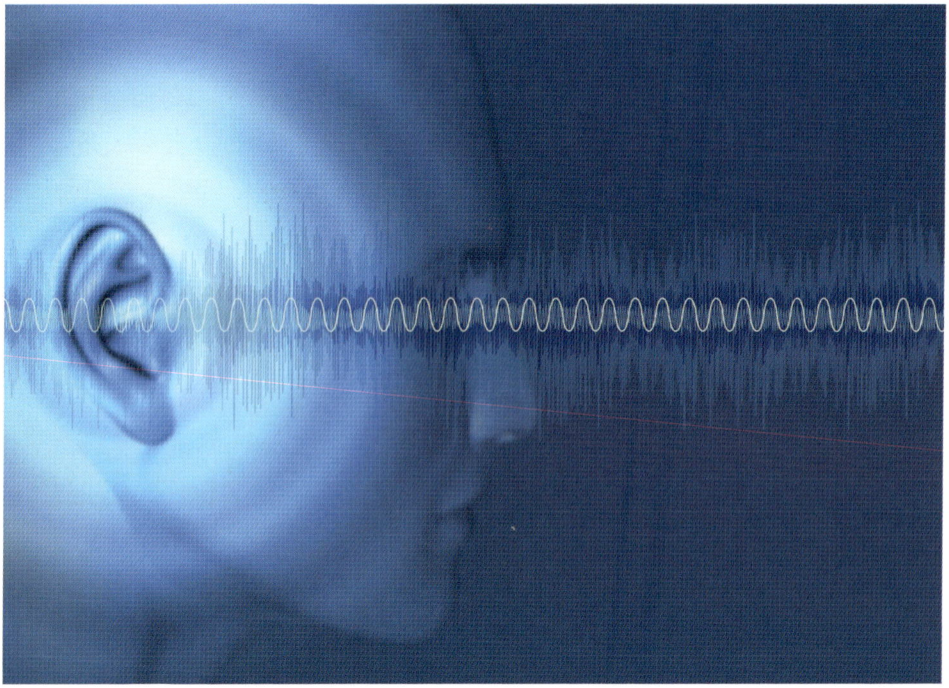

Exercise 1: **Listening**

What is sound? Well, it all depends on how you look at it. Have you ever heard the sound of a computer or fax machine on your telephone line? It's all hissing and crackling, and yet masses of information are passing through with that sound. Imagine that our communication technology was advanced by another 100 years and you could pass the amount of genetic code information required to build a complete human being down the phone line every second. What would the sound of that be?

Imagine the tone of a crystal bowl or glass ringing sweetly, or even the harmony of thousands of crystal tones making beautiful music. I propose that these are the types of sounds you may eventually hear in meditation, if you listen well. It has been coined 'holy sound' by some in the Sikh religion, but we are going to call it 'healing sound'.

Just sit and listen to this sound inside your head. In the beginning, it will sound like a very high-pitched whistle. It may be like a tiny crystal glass ringing or the electrical sound of something like a television or computer going in the other room, or perhaps many microscopic summer cicadas singing. That almost ultrasonic frequency of sound is what I suggest listening to. You might even think you have a case of tinnitus, but if you listen deep into it you will soon realise it is something else entirely. It has a deep penetrating feeling that comes with it. It comes with a healing energy if you accept it into your energy field. By listening to it and tuning in to this sound you will find that your intuition becomes clearer, your hearing becomes better and your ability to think and process information is greatly increased.

This inner 'healing sound' may be the quickest, simplest and clearest connection to healing energy you can make, and may in fact carry genetic information. It can also help you identify subtle signals from your higher intuition or guidance from above. I suggest this because this sound fits within the realm of the universal information highway, similar to that discussed earlier. We can all hear it to varying degrees, and increasing awareness of this type of sound often precedes personal spiritual experiences, which we will talk more about soon. Listening will open your sixth sense and increase your 'still, small voice' within (the voice of your higher intuition, the voice of the spirit, or the voice of God). Eventually, you can practise meditative listening anytime at all, even stuck in traffic, standing in a queue or sitting in a waiting room, or any place that provides an appropriate moment.

All you need to do is sit, listen, and listen some more. You may enjoy the feelings that come with it. Once your mind starts to wander, try the next exercise, which focuses on looking. To start with you should find 5–10 minutes of listening is enough.

Exercise 2: **Looking**

What is light? In relation to meditation, the term 'light' may be used in reference to many things, such as electricity, starlight, inner light, spiritual illumination, guiding light or a force for good.

There really are no finite boundaries on light, only to the degree to which we can measure it. Light becomes invisible at a certain point and it can reach massive speeds and be of an infinitely small size. For example, gamma rays pass directly through our planet, and they are simply a very high-frequency form of light. Once again we are seeing the great mystery of the energy in our universe. Dark energy itself may, in theory, be visible light, through different eyes in the spiritual realm. Science still debates whether light is a particle or a wave, but concludes that it could be both, a bit like a type of EM/plasma combination. In other words, it could be a finer form of matter than we can currently experience — almost pre-matter, but still matter.

Consider your dreams, for example, which can sometimes appear very vivid and real. We can feel things in our dreams, and these feelings can be very real, especially our emotions. The pineal gland in our brain produces a natural chemical hallucinogen called N-dimethyltryptamine (DMT). Interestingly the pineal gland contains retinal cells, such as photoreceptors, similar to our eyes. Does this explain why hallucinations are often seen as real, because we are actually seeing into another realm, or seeing through a third eye?

Tests have shown that people who take synthetic DMT report a feeling of transcending their body and entering into an alternative 'realm'; an audible perception of a high pitched whining/whirring sound during the onset of the experience; perceiving and communicating with 'presences' or 'entities'; plus reflections on death, dying and the after-life. In addition, the reported vividness of these subjective experiences has led to near-death experiences, and DMT users describing the states they enter as 'realer than real'.[5]

Because DMT appears to be primarily synthesised in the pineal gland, which is right in the centre of your head, and because science has yet to resolve the biochemical mechanisms by which the hallucinogens (psychedelics) dramatically alter perception and consciousness, the process of waking 'visions' and sleeping 'dreams'[6] remains a great mystery.

This poses the question: do we actually have a third or spiritual eye? This question supplies another powerful exercise for meditation, namely, looking. I suggest trying the following exercise.

Simply sit in a quiet place and find something about five paces away, maybe the wall opposite or the ceiling, if you are lying down. This works best in the dark. Now slowly close your eyes while continuing to look at the distance of the far wall or ceiling. It is important to remain focused at that distance so you keep looking. Actually, the further away you can focus, the better. You can even look at the distance of the night sky while lying on the ground.

What you are looking for is light or colours of any description. The longer you look, the more you will potentially find — and you may be surprised at what you see. This exercise may improve eyesight and it will help you keep occupied if you're doing the listening meditation and find your mind is wandering.[7]

At first, you may see thousands of tiny small dots and the occasional twinkling light. You might begin to see bright balls of light, patterns of energy, beautiful lifelike moving patterns of light, moon or star-like objects, or even spiritual visions. Don't be disappointed if you don't see anything at all. This meditation is a bit like learning to play the piano; it takes time, but you have no lessons to take, as you simply need to practise looking for a few minutes a day and keep an open mind.

If you are lucky enough to see wonderful lights or perhaps even visions then I need say no more. Try both looking and listening at the same time to get the best experience. You will find that the sound and light are connected. If and when you do start hearing and seeing things, don't think you've gone mad. You're just opening the doorway to a higher state of awareness, and this is how you can connect very powerfully to the healing energy.

After a while, you may get tired of this exercise. You can then move on to the next exercise, which is based around feeling. This is the big kahuna — the king of awareness when it comes to healing energy.

Exercise 3: **Feeling**

What is feeling? This is a very interesting question since we can actually feel sound, heat, light, air, water, and emotions, and even mental impressions can be felt.

What you can do with this meditation is allow yourself to feel the energy moving into, around, and even through your body. If you hold no rigid belief system, stay humble, and purely have an open mind; you will be able to experience the full healing effects offered by this practice. If you have doubts or negative thoughts while doing this you will not achieve the benefits, so it is essential to focus on loving, kind thoughts and be in the highest possible moral position, mentally and emotionally, when you start. I always ask myself to be open to only the highest good and take the universal, unconditional loving perspective that we talked about in earlier chapters.

Enter into the listening and looking meditation for a few minutes and then begin really focusing on what you can feel. It can be very powerful or it can be very gentle. It all depends on what you need at the time. The forces of nature and the energy of healing will always bring you the required response. You may feel warmth, tingling, buzzing, humming, coolness, lightness, spacey, floating sensations and many, many more feelings. Sometimes you may shake, tremble or convulse. This is all okay; let it happen naturally, and it will pass. Above all else, as time passes you may feel a lasting feeling of divine love and peace.

If you feel this then you have made the greatest of all discoveries you can make with meditation! You have discovered your true self, the very essence of what you are made of, and what it is that makes you. This divine universal love comes as a combination of light, sound and a feeling of gentle bliss within. It is made of subtle EM plasma and information and has the power to heal you on all levels. It contains the fullness of all knowledge there is to know, and yet it shares itself with you as a feeling. Once you have found this feeling, you have the ability to transform any negative state into a positive state, whether it be physical, mental or emotional. Once you have located your connection with the great spiritual energy of universal love, you have found your unconditional healing energy and can connect with it at will.

The mind may step in the way, but we will come back and deal with that possibility in depth a little later. There is no point in attempting to place your experiences within a belief system but rather build your library of knowledge around your direct personal experiences. This way you can remain completely open to limitless new experiences and can continue to grow and progress.

Transformational healing is exactly that, a process of profound change deep within one's energy field at an eternal soul level. This simple meditation method summarised again below will help open you up to this growth and change, and equally, it will allow your physical body to positively respond to these changes.

A fixed belief system simply can't contain these new experiences, but your true knowledge built from experimentation may endlessly expand and remain flexible enough to accommodate infinite new experiences. Otherwise, you simply miss out on many of the possible experiences offered by this meditation practice. You must leave yourself open to discover and experience what great infinite realities meditation offers, because if there is one absolute certainty in the universe, it is this: everything must grow, change and transform.

Meditation method summary

1. Find a quiet comfortable place without music or any outer disturbance. Get comfortable.
2. Take several slow, deep breaths and then simply rest.
3. Do the listening exercise for 5–10 minutes.
4. Move on to the looking exercise for 5–10 minutes.
5. Then focus on the feeling exercise for 5–10 minutes.
6. Try combining all three exercises for 5–10 minutes.
7. Stop and rest for 5 minutes.
8. Repeat the above as often as you feel comfortable.
9. Allow some time afterward for stillness and reflection.
10. Increase your time as comfortable, eventually aiming for an hour or longer.

By creating a quiet space for observation you will have opened up a channel and this naturally allows energy to move, by the law of simple diffusion. No effort is required. This is simply a process of observation.

By now you should have a reasonably clear understanding of the nature of healing energy, where it comes from, how it moves, how to connect with it, and also how to tap into it.

In the next chapter, we are going to get this energy moving through your body. The initial experiences with healing energy can be wonderful and uncomplicated, but as we progress the energy will start to work on us and we require some understanding of the healing process to facilitate more complete healing in the body, mind and emotions.

I hope this gets you started and underway today with your practice of self-healing. We are about to start using this healing energy in a more specific fashion in the coming chapters.

My story continues . . .

During my mid-twenties, as my studies continued and my meditations become more lengthy, I also found myself experiencing a major break-up of my second long-term relationship, with a deep sense of failure. I moved into a small flat on my own and poured myself into my work. I then injured my back at my labouring job and was put on accident compensation for two years. This turn of events allowed me to spend my days working with herbal medicine, self-healing and meditation full time. I tried fasting, detoxing and started reading about herbal detoxing, nutrition, Chinese medicine, Buddhism, the Kabbalah, the Bible and any other books I could find on the subjects of health and enlightenment. One night after fasting on only oranges for 10 days, I woke in the middle of the night to an out-of-body/in-body experience, where I felt my body was weightless, and my brain was being softly blown with a type of electromagnetic wind. I could both feel it and hear it, just like my head was a hollow wind

tunnel. It was an incredible energy experience I will never forget, and I put it down entirely to the combination of fasting and meditation. Each day I would meditate for up to four hours, and often I would go and sit under a tree in the bush walk just outside my flat. About two years of doing this consistently gave me probably the greatest vision of energy I have ever experienced. I was sitting under this large tree where I had been meditating every day, and I was looking into the twilight sky. All of a sudden I was lifted above myself into the air, out of my body, and yet I could still feel my body as well. This was very weird. I was in two separate positions simultaneously. At that very moment an object appeared in the sky, about the size of the moon. I could not tell the distance, but it was beyond the clouds, and it could have been in space, but as this was not part of our physical reality, distance seemed irrelevant. The object was made of light and it was constructed of multiple spinning geometric shapes, one within the other. (In later years I learnt that these are what's called the platonic solids.) Emanating from this object was a spherical wave, similar to how circular ripples travel on water when a stone is dropped, except these waves were three-dimensional spheres. The waves came out from the object all the way down to the earth. I felt like I was literally picked up by them. I felt them tangibly, and I also began to feel myself undulate like I was floating on water in a small boat as the gentle waves passed through me. I looked around and saw the waves were also penetrating the trees and everything else around me. It consciously struck me that this could be some kind of energy mechanism, sending subatomic information through our world as subtle electromagnetic energy. This was one possible explanation. The experience lasted for only a couple of minutes and quickly faded, but this

vision will never leave my mind as personal proof that we are not the only dimension of reality, and that science can never observe or understand everything. In my brief state of higher consciousness I struggled to observe this phenomenon for more than a short time. Again, this window only opened up to me because I was honestly searching, humble, and had simplified my mind and body through fasting and meditation. Since that day I still occasionally feel those waves around me, but it happens unexpectedly and only for about 30 seconds at any given time. I have never really given this a detailed examination, but I am certain what I saw was real and it exists for a great purpose. I feel perhaps it's part of a great network of energy/information transmission highways throughout the universe, and was put there intentionally. I'm not sharing this for any other reason than to get you excited about the possibilities of meditation. It really can change your life.

Chapter 7:

The simplicity principle

The key that opens the door to healing energy flow is actually not hard to find. It's just that sometimes the most obvious thing is the very thing we overlook, like how the trees impede our view of the forest. The answer to our problem can be right in front of us, staring us in the face, but we're looking beyond it for something more advanced or complex. Oftentimes less is actually more. Welcome to the power of simplicity!

A great example of simplicity versus complexity can be seen in the atom. If you compare hydrogen to plutonium, hydrogen has only one proton and one electron, while plutonium has 94 of each. The energy from hydrogen is therefore much more freely available than the energy from plutonium. We can simply light a match and trigger the release of energy from hydrogen, but we need a nuclear power plant and a massive particle accelerator to get the energy to release from within a plutonium atom.

The simple element of hydrogen is consequently much lighter and floats in the atmosphere, while plutonium must be mined from within the earth. When you look at the elements used by all living creatures in the processes of life, they are the most simple. These include hydrogen, oxygen, nitrogen and carbon. The reason is that these simple elements

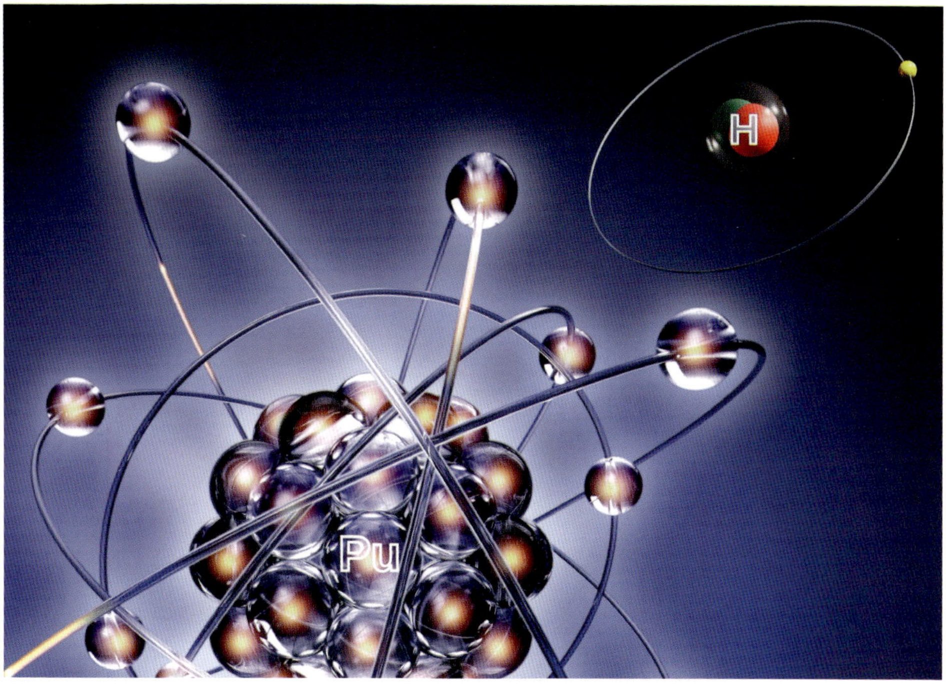

easily liberate energy, share, and exchange parts, and can easily be built into a wide range of structures. It's the simple elements our body uses for healing, while the heavier elements, such as lead, are the most toxic to our body.

Even our DNA is made from those light, simple elements. You could say that when we come into the world, we're also very simple in nature. We have no attitudes, beliefs or opinions, and therefore information is both received and transmitted by our DNA very clearly. The only interference we have at this stage has come from our parents' pattern of energy.

As we get older, things gradually get more complicated, and we start to react to the various difficulties that life presents. It's our responses and the mechanisms that we use to cope with the inevitable stresses of life that are largely responsible for complicating and confusing the cellular communication in our body. You could say that our attitudes, opinions, beliefs, world view, coping mechanisms and other constructs that we put in place interfere with the pure simple healing messages that we received in the beginning, via our DNA.

The common expressions 'I felt like I was carrying the weight of the world on my shoulders' or 'He left with a heavy heart' denote the feelings we have when life has become a little too complex for our liking. Complex situations bring a burden upon us. In contrast, simple times lighten our mood and bring us joy. Our health and healing process is no different. Healing should not require complex methods (rocket science) but should be simple, creating space and time, thus allowing our body to bounce back to health naturally.

People who lead a simpler life, such as those living on islands or in smaller towns, appear to have fewer of the complex health issues that people suffer from in highly populated areas, like the big cities. The simpler life is the healthier life, and keeping it simple may be the most powerful tool when it comes to self-healing. Not only does it create space for more energy to flow, but it may also encourage better communication within the body's network hormonally, neurologically and genetically.

One of the best ways to achieve this is through the meditation practice that we spoke about in the last chapter. Another way to simplify the processes internally is to perform a detox or cleanse on the physical level, simplifying our digestive process and purifying our body chemistry. We will talk about this more in the chapters to come.

Complexity invites dis-ease, while simplicity brings peace and health to the body and mind. In other words, as the old saying goes, 'Keep it simple, stupid' — or as I like to say, 'Keep it simple, genius'. Let me explain how this can be applied in our everyday lives.

Classic examples of 'Keeping it simple'

Complex: Drive around the block four times in a traffic jam looking for a parking space right outside the door of your destination.
Simple: Take the first parking spot you see within a one-block radius of your destination and walk there.

Complex: Fight your way to the top of your profession, working massive amounts of overtime to achieve wealth, status, power and possessions.
Simple: Do what you love, to help others and follow your dreams.

Complex: Go to the gym, pay a trainer, get a personal programme and work out for 10 hours a week.
Simple: Go for a 20-minute walk twice a week, get plenty of fresh air, sunlight and water, and eat well.

Complex: Go to every doctor, health practitioner, and health store, spending thousands of dollars trying dozens of natural health products and therapies to try and feel better.
Simple: Complete a detox programme once every year, learn about self-healing, and make one small improvement to simplify your lifestyle annually.

How complexity invites disease

What makes you immediately feel sick to your stomach? A new pile of paperwork thrown onto your desk, being stuck in a traffic jam, getting put on hold on your phone for hours, waiting in a long queue, or the many financial challenges we face as adults, including the long forms you have to fill out at the bank or tax department? All of these things represent complexity in life and that causes us frustration. It feels like you're being blocked and your energy starts to bottle up.

That's because we're much happier when life is simple. You don't see many animals having a nervous breakdown or falling into depression. Their lives are much simpler and therefore they are generally much

healthier. It's exactly the same principle with our food and medicine. The golden rule of health has got to be 'Keep it simple'.

Clear examples of complexity-related diseases include stress, anxiety, depression, digestive disturbances, eating disorders and metabolic imbalances, which can all be caused by the frustrating, painful aspects of life. When you are also exposed to chemicals, additives, pollution, radiation, drugs, junk foods, alcohol, sugar, red meats and other acid-forming protein foods, it becomes very hard for your body to deal with everyday levels of mental and emotional stress.

You can see how complicated life can become and how quickly it can begin to erode your health. As the body and mind struggle to process everything that's thrown at them, the burden can eventually take you down. In contrast, it's the pure and simple things that heal.

How simplicity heals

If you look at any great success story or 'genius' solution to a problem, it always comes back to the principle of simplification. A classic example is Albert Einstein's $E = mc^2$. This simple formula applies to all energy and matter in the universe.

Every advance in technology is actually a step of simplification creating ease, because the more we understand the laws and principles behind things and apply those laws, the simpler life becomes. Ultimately, the answers to any problem should be the simplest.

There is a famous principle called Occam's razor. It is most commonly described as 'the simplest answer is most often correct', but the accurate interpretation is actually 'entities should not be multiplied needlessly', i.e., researchers should avoid stacking information to prove a theory if a simpler explanation fits the observations.

Simplicity in health

The same principle applies to all aspects of life, especially when it comes to health and healing. I can't emphasise this enough, especially to those of you who already are, or are looking at becoming, health professionals. Don't lose sight of the forest for the trees.

One common mistake a lot of people make when they start applying mainstream medicine or even 'alternative' traditional and natural medicine is to overthink and overkill things with details. The complexity of this approach can defeat the purpose entirely and create more stress, worry and confusion than was present at the beginning. Many natural health practitioners and even healers make this very same mistake. The answer is not complex, it's simple. Plants and animals survive in the wild with no human intervention, and often despite human interference.

By performing a detox programme we simplify what we put into our body by consuming only whole, unprocessed plant foods. This allows a simple digestive process, and that frees up a lot of extra time and energy for your body to perform its natural healing functions.

Love heals the heart, but also the body. You can show somebody your love in many ways, any of which can encourage healing. I have practised energy healing for many years and the simple fact is that compassion, empathy, love and simple touch can help heal the body of another. Sometimes that's all it takes. A most simple truth.

From this observation, I have also seen that light, air, water and simple food can all do the same thing. They contain healing powers because they are simple and they follow basic universal principles of life. They are attuned to the universal intelligence, conveyed via the

EM/plasma field, and they remind our bodies of the simple basic laws of living energy. Herbal medicines are the same — they are pure, natural, and have healing power.

You can see the power of simplicity in many examples throughout the world of religion, spiritual practices, and healing arts. It's when man-made complications arise from the simple beginnings that the core messages of these methods can get lost. We have a tendency to overcomplicate things, to our detriment.

Every atom, molecule, particle and substance essentially has logical, mathematical, predictable ways of behaving and interacting, which means everything follows a predetermined order or pattern and is not performing some sort of random, chaotic behaviour. This is exemplified in the science of chemistry and physics. Those exact same rules apply to our internal energy on the physical, emotional and mental levels.

We often use the term 'mental complex' for a psychological disorder and 'baggage' for an emotional problem. Even within the healing arts the term 'energy blockage' is commonly used. We instinctively know that what's going on is a form of complexity that is adding weight and internal stress to our energy field. The inner communication network is disrupted, and our connection to the loving, unconditional healing energy is clouded. This causes us to feel pain on many levels, eventually leading to the disease process if not resolved.

If we want to lighten our load, interact freely, and experience all the various possibilities in our lives then we need to make our energy field more like the simple elements of life, such as hydrogen, oxygen, nitrogen and carbon. We need to become part of the simple living breathing energy of life itself.

To do this we must simplify our process on all levels, including physical, emotional and mental. So remember . . .

Complexity invites dis-ease, while simplicity encourages healing.

Complexity
Invites Disease

A symbolic cross-section of the human energy field from above

Characteristic Feelings

Heavy, cold, disturbed, sad, tired, painful and stressed

Simplicity
Encourages Healing
A symbolic cross-section of the human energy field from above
A pure heart and an open mind
Absolute universal truth
Liberated Energy
Pure Healing Information
Reaches all parts of the body and beyond
Characteristic Feelings
Light, warm, peaceful, happy, energetic, pleasurable and comforting

My story continues . . .

I had an experience of simplicity in my late twenties when living alone for a few months in a top-floor apartment. I was studying herbal medicine and reading many books on medicine and healing. I was also experimenting more with food and trying a clean diet and a little fasting. In the evenings I would make stir-fry from fresh vegetables, some curry, chilli or tomatoes, and have this with brown rice. I would then walk down to the beach to sit and meditate on the rocks. Getting right down where the water was crashing against the boulders, I would find a big rock I could sit on. I would spend an hour or two sitting there just meditating, listening and looking within my mind. The sound of the sea was all-encompassing and completely calmed my mind. I did this consistently every night, along with the whole food, for six weeks. Then one evening I walked back to my apartment and entered the kitchen area. There was a dark brown plastic concertina door between the kitchen and bathroom, with no windows in the kitchen. The lights were turned off in the kitchen as it was twilight and just getting dark. As I walked in, I noticed a faint glow coming from the bathroom through the concertina door. I just rested there for a second and suddenly the solid wall next to the concertina door started to move like it was transparent. Small bright lights started to appear, almost like fireflies, except they were about the size of marbles. To my surprise they were coming down through the wall on a 45-degree angle, spinning in little circles, and then going back upwards. The longer I watched the further I could see, until it was like I was looking up into the sky above my apartment. There were hundreds of these firefly-like balls of light and they were dancing in beautiful patterns in harmony with each other. They had tails like little comets and would come down, then shoot back up very quickly. I sat there for what must have been 5–10 minutes watching this energy dance. It was so bright and clear that I know it had nothing to do with anything man-made and was not of this three-dimensional material world. This was no hallucination; I had literally seen into another dimension. From that point forward my belief in the world beyond moved on from being just a belief, and became what I call 'absolute knowledge'. I could never doubt the 'other side' was right there, just beyond our perception. I had seen it. I had witnessed something out of a science fiction movie, but it was real. I thought about this experience later and realised it must have been due to my consistent fasting and meditation for those previous six weeks. I had simplified myself both physically and mentally, so my process was pure, which had removed the veil from my mind and opened my eyes. Once again, my experimentation had paid dividends. But how was I going to use this new information? Only the future would tell.

Chapter 8:

Channelling space

Health is a state of peace found when the body, mind and spirit resonate in perfect harmony. This sounds like a bit of a mystical principle, but really it comes down to the first thing you learn on day one when studying human anatomy and physiology, and that's what's called 'homeostasis'. I want you to understand this principle because finding peace is what health and healing are all about.

So what is homeostasis? The *Encyclopaedia Britannica* explains it like this:

> *Any self-regulating process by which biological systems tend to maintain stability while adjusting to conditions that are optimal for survival. If homeostasis is successful, life continues; if unsuccessful, disaster or death ensues. The stability attained is actually a dynamic equilibrium, in which continuous change occurs yet relatively uniform conditions prevail.*
>
> *Any system in dynamic equilibrium tends to reach a steady-state, a balance that resists outside forces of change. When such a system is disturbed, built-in regulatory devices respond to the departures to establish a new balance; such a process is one of feedback control. All processes of integration and coordination of function, whether mediated by electrical circuits or by nervous and hormonal systems, are examples of homeostatic regulation.*[1]

Healing works in exactly the same way. By accepting, channelling and integrating the informational healing energy, we enable balance, peace and homeostasis to occur within us on all levels. In saying that, you can only channel healing energy when the energy encounters some space into which it can be received. It's hard to hear your friend talking to you across a room full of noisy people at a party, and you can't park your car in a carpark building that is full. Healing energy responds in a like manner. It can't move in or communicate when the space is noisy and busy. This applies on all levels, mental, emotional and physical.

The hydropower dam is another great example. If water levels were equal on both sides of the dam, then when you opened the flood gates nothing would happen. It's exactly the same within the human body. Because healing energy is contained within an infinite reservoir and is completely unconditional, it's always ready to be released and poured down upon us, or, more correctly, pass through our energy field.

A noisy, crowded, busy or crammed-full situation, where no space is available, is not going to allow anything new to be introduced. As we've established, health is a state of peace and harmony — and yet space needs to be made available for healing energy to move and communicate, so we need to achieve both quietude and space.

The reservoir

To give a little scientific reference to my claim of an infinite universal energy reservoir, let's consider what's called the cosmic microwave background (CMB). It consists of the energy in the microwave portion of the electromagnetic spectrum, which emits heat — about 2.725°K on the Kelvin scale. It fills the entire universe uniformly and can be detected everywhere we look with our telescopes. In fact, if we could see microwaves, the entire sky would glow with a brightness that was astonishingly uniform in every direction. Scientists claim that this CMB is evidence of the 'Big Bang Theory', but mysteriously, it does not seem to originate from any particular direction, which leaves them a little confused.[2] If there was a big bang, then surely the CMB would be hotter in one direction or another, but it's exactly the same temperature everywhere.

Microwaves are also the type of electromagnetic energy we use to transmit information at the speed of light. They are very fast and highly effective at carrying massive amounts of information long distances. Even back in 2011, we were able to send up to 20 gigabytes per second via microwave satellites.[3]

I did say we had an infinite reservoir of universal consciousness and healing energy, which contains all the information we need for life. Well, that's exactly what we have just described, an infinite unconditional reservoir of healing energy, which carries information and is always ready to pour 'down upon' and 'out from' within us.

What I'm trying to say here is, perhaps instead of a theoretical Big Bang, we have an infinite field of energy, information and intelligence that is continuously creating our universe from a higher subtle-matter dimension. Surely, that would explain the consistent nature of the CMB and also shed light on what the mysterious universal dark matter and energy may consist of, i.e. a blend of EM, plasma/matter and consciousness.

In order for us to maintain health and perfect balance, healing energy needs to be flowing continuously through the channels within us and those channels can be broken down into very simple levels.

In earlier chapters we've talked about energy flow, resonating, connecting and simplifying, but just as water needs to flow to stay clean, pure healing energy needs to go through us in order to keep us healthy and clean. Water will accumulate sediment, algae and scum when stagnant, and the same thing occurs with stagnant healing energy. If it's not flowing through us and being released in a creative way then it causes pain, stress and eventually disease.

Our energy field and consciousness act just like a drop of water in a great endless ocean of cosmic microwave energy, EM/plasma, and consciousness, which extends throughout the entire universe. Plus, our energy field and consciousness are part of an infinite creative force that needs to flow. In other words, we need to channel this energy in a creative way in order for it to freely flow through us. We already talked about the vertical one-way energy exchange, and how energy needs to flow in one direction from above, and into the physical world unconditionally. But how can we make this happen easily?

Consider how water cascades down a terraced waterfall. In the same way, healing energy cascades down through the levels of our being. We've all heard about body, mind and spirit, but the levels I'm talking about here are slightly different: they are the mental, emotional and physical. The spirit we include as an interwoven part of the healing energy reservoir in this instance. You can see these levels clarified in the diagram opposite.

These levels make a channel for the energy to flow from the top down, from the reservoir of healing energy down into our brain (or mind), then into our visceral emotions, and then out into our physical body. Eventually, this energy exits our body and is released as heat or goes into the ground electrically. Either way, this is a grounding process, and grounding is a very important part of this creative channelling process.

A key thing to remember here is that just like the universe is continually expanding and new worlds are being created, we must do the same. Our consciousness is integrated with the universal consciousness and also needs to create. Our energy will be released in the correct one-way energy flow as previously described when we actively participate in a creative endeavour with love. Because healing energy is unconditional it requires us to cooperate and become part of the loving creative process that is taking place throughout the entire universe. To integrate body, mind and spirit (which is the purpose of life on earth) we must learn to drop our ego and join in with the infinite process of universal creativity. Let's take a step back and look at this in a little more detail.

From the top down the energy levels are as follows.

- Unconditional healing energy — The infinite reservoir (universal consciousness/spirit)
- Mental — Our brain and mind
- Emotional — Our gut instinct and our feelings
- Physical — Our body metabolism, tissues and muscles
- Ground — Either heat or electrical grounding

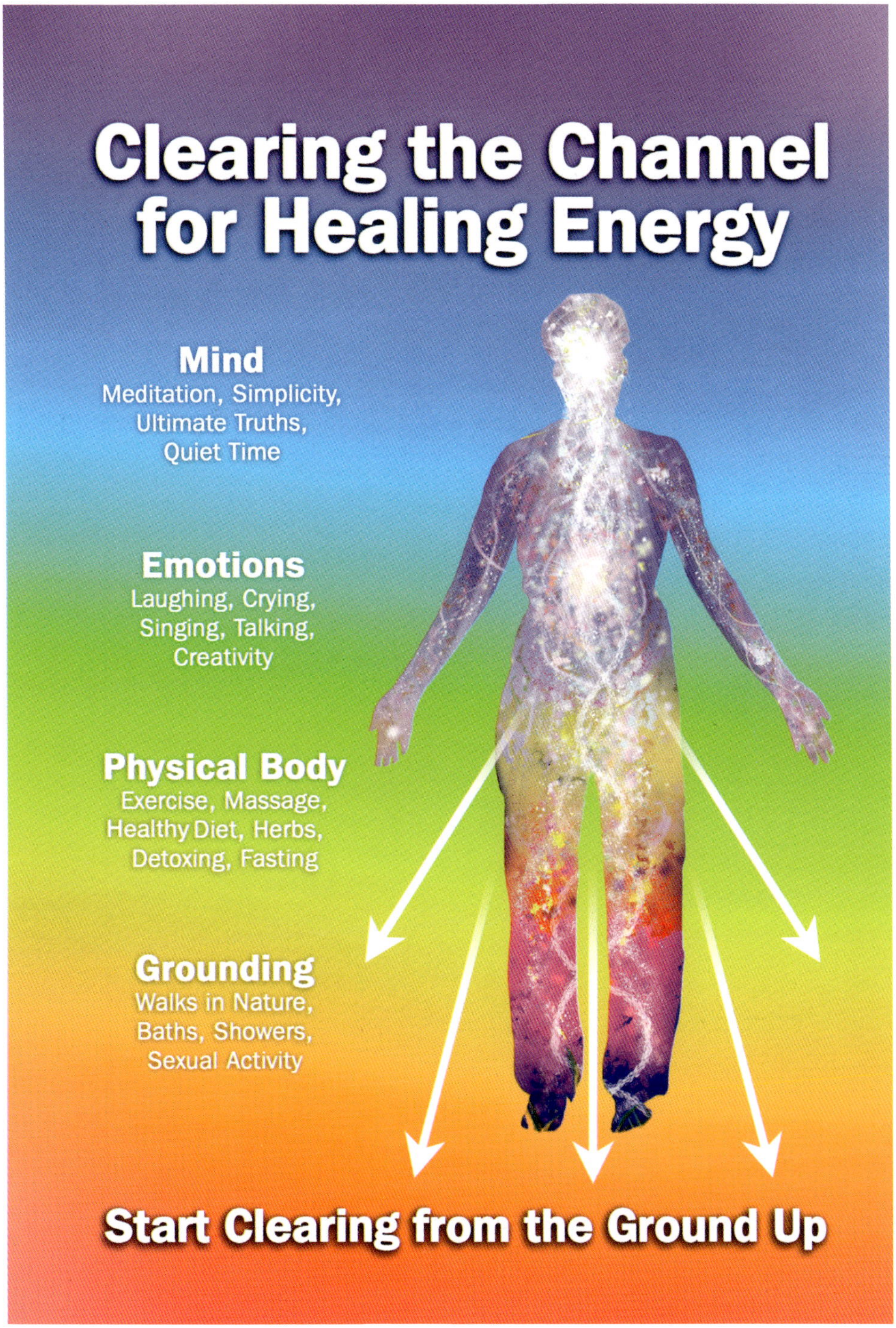
Clearing the Channel for Healing Energy
Mind
Meditation, Simplicity, Ultimate Truths, Quiet Time
Emotions
Laughing, Crying, Singing, Talking, Creativity
Physical Body
Exercise, Massage, Healthy Diet, Herbs, Detoxing, Fasting
Grounding
Walks in Nature, Baths, Showers, Sexual Activity
Start Clearing from the Ground Up

As with any energy or transport system, if there is confusion, resistance or complexity somewhere along the way it creates a bottle-neck, and a back-up occurs. This causes frustration, stress and pain. More often than not, this occurs within us on the emotional and mental levels, causing physical pain and eventually disease.

It's almost always our ego and its false opinions, attitudes, beliefs and defence mechanisms that cause these problems. Dropping these is possibly the most powerful thing we can do to open the channel. Practising meditation regularly is one of the quickest ways to achieve this, because once we start to have new experiences our eyes and ears are opened, our hearts are humbled, our ego drops, and we begin to feel true bliss and happiness.

Our blockages, pains and frustrations can be let go and dissolved into finer materials that we can easily eliminate. It all passes away effortlessly and is released from the body as metabolic waste and heat. The illustration on the previous page demonstrates how that inner energy channel might look, and what we can do to clear the way for healing energy to flow.

Healing by diffusion

A classic example of homeostasis in action is diffusion. If you consume too much salt your body will attempt to dilute the salt in order to maintain a steady electrolyte balance. It will do this by retaining water. If you drink sea water, your kidneys will try and get rid of the salt. The human kidneys can only make urine that is less salty than sea water. Therefore, to get rid of all the excess salt taken in by drinking sea water, you have to urinate more water than you drink. Eventually, you would die of dehydration, all the while becoming more and more thirsty.

This is what your body does with everything it takes on, including emotions, thoughts, beliefs and food. A common mistake we make as human beings is this: we think if we get more energy from the world around us, we will feel fulfilled and happy. In fact, the opposite happens to us: we feel more and more drained as we look to the world around us for fulfilment. Our worldly desires behave like sea water, and our thirst is never quenched.

What we tend to do is get more and more busy as a result, trying to accumulate as much worldly energy as possible. We accumulate worldly energy in the form of possessions. Too many possessions and you become a hoarder, which begins to block the flow of energy in your life. Materialism/consumerism is basically salt water to the soul.

The same applies on an emotional level. People who want a lot of emotional energy from the world around them become very needy, almost like energy parasites to those around them, leaving everyone feeling drained and abused. That selfish kind of emotional entrapment can cause blockages in energy flow.

The same can be said about the mental level, with addictions to violent gaming and movies, abusive social media and all kinds of negative mental noise. Along with this comes worry, doubts, anxiety, fear and negativity. Somehow this never-ending mental chatter becomes addictive and unstoppable, which eventually leads to mental stress. As the proverb reminds us: 'As a man thinketh in his heart, so is he' (Proverbs 23:7).

When we're looking into the world on the horizontal plane for our energy, it will never truly satisfy us. What we need in order to open the channel for healing energy is quite the opposite of all of this. We need to create space for the energy to flow, and to do that we must find a quiet place of peace.

We need to stop, look, listen, feel and appreciate the beauty around us in every moment. Find space and quiet, content in understanding that this world is like salt water and will never bring us lasting happiness. Only giving and sharing the unconditional love and healing that comes from above will give us peace and health.

The law of conservation of energy

In physics, the law of conservation of energy states that the total energy of an isolated system remains constant and is conserved over time. Energy can neither be created nor destroyed; rather, it transforms from one form to another.[4]

Ultimately, healing energy is shared between these various levels of ourselves in an attempt to find balance and harmony. Therefore, we need to address them all in order to get healing energy to move. The equation is: **Spirit** = **Mind** = **Emotions** = **Body** = **Creation**.

In order for energy to flow between these levels from the infinite reservoir above, we need to make space. Just like opening the flood gates, we need to start at the bottom level, the physical. It's no good opening the flood gates upstream or there will most definitely be a bottleneck somewhere down the line. We need to first open the channels where the energy finally exits. That will get things moving in the right direction without causing any discomfort.

I know this is getting a little heavy but I'm getting to the point shortly. Let's summarise what we've learnt.

- There is an infinite reservoir of universal healing energy above the level of our minds.
- Your body will always try to balance itself to bring you back to a healthy state (homeostasis).
- Both your mental and emotional state are affected by the functions of your body, as they are closely intertwined.
- To get the flow of healing energy started we need to create a quiet, still, open, and empty space.
- It's better to start creating this space at the lowest end of our energy levels, then energy will naturally flow down the channel unimpeded.

What does this all actually mean? In a nutshell, it means that to achieve effective channelling of energy without causing disruption to homeostatic balance, we must follow a logical step-by-step procedure. I will outline these steps for you now.

Step 1: **Clear the physical level**
This is most commonly done by detoxing, cleansing and fasting. Practised for thousands of years by many religions and spiritual practices, detoxing, cleansing and fasting help us to detach from drawing energy from the physical world around us. It encourages us to draw on the energies from above, to look inwards, towards the spirit, rather than continually scoffing more and more food. Other things you do to encourage the physical release of energy are: creative endeavours, short bursts of strenuous exercise, sexual activity, massage, spa treatments and other body therapy techniques. You get the idea.

Step 2: **Clear the emotional level**
Once we start to detach from sourcing energy from the physical world and worldly substances around us and start to connect with the energy from above, we may start to experience what is commonly called 'withdrawal symptoms'. This often causes needy, emotional energy to come to the surface, which is good. It makes us aware of our error. We need to release this emotional energy now that we have a clear channel on the physical level. It's good to sing, dance, laugh, cry, yell and even scream (maybe in the car or into a pillow). This emotional energy needs to be accepted, acknowledged and released so we can move on to the next level. Try not to blame anyone else for how you're feeling. It's temporary and it's okay. Remember, it's just energy and it will all end up as heat eventually.

Step 3: **Clear the mind**
Now we have cleared a channel below, clearing the mind will be a lot easier. This is not to say it will be without incident, but at least we have created emotional space for our mental downstream flow. People often comment when they do a detox and cleansing programme that they

start feeling more emotional peace and mental clarity. This is a great bonus of detoxing and cleansing the body physically, similar to calming the dirty waters after a storm. After a few days of detoxing the waters become still and clear again, and the light is able to shine through. This is a great time to employ the meditation method that we spoke about in chapter 6.

If our thoughts are mostly of this world, temporal, and wrapped up in physical gratification, then it is unlikely we are considering our spirit first, and centering our life around its eternal plan. Constantly looking for temporary satisfaction and gratification on the mental, emotional and physical levels will put us out of balance with our eternal spirit, the most powerful part of ourselves, from where healing energy emanates.

The key thing to remember here is that in order to channel the energy we need to create space at the furthest exit point. In other words, we need to start at ground level and work our way up, literally. There is absolutely no point trying to force energy upwards or inwards back towards the source. Energy also will not move into, down, or out into a congested space. We simply can't channel energy when there's not a clear channel available.

Once this channel has been cleared correctly, energy will naturally start to flow, so long as we are tuned in and resonating with the source of energy, as we spoke about earlier. Channelling energy then becomes entirely effortless.

In the next chapter, we will talk about how we can use our mind more specifically, and following that, how we can use our hands to manipulate this energy and encourage healing in our bodies to specific areas.

My story continues . . .

My previous experiences had shown me how simplifying my process had opened up a channel within me to receive energy. Yes, mostly I had seen, felt and realised that there was a universal energy available to us. I had sometimes been almost paralysed by the power of this energy entering my body. Perhaps this was due to my previous bad habits of smoking, drinking, eating lots of meat and heavily processed foods, including massive amounts of sugar. My body had been detoxing and healing simultaneously and the energy shifts were profound. As part of my journey, physical healing began to take place. First my back pain was relieved and there was hope that I may not need the surgery that was suggested. In fact, my back has healed completely. Itchy dry rashes I had on my body, which could have been partly due to the processed foods, had disappeared, and I was slowly overcoming my addictive tendencies. This took several years to be completely free, but I can testify, healing energy can help you overcome any addiction. The greatest blessing I can share is that my ability to truly love somebody and hold a long-term healthy relationship was being restored. Not to say there were no bumps in the road, as I'm now in my third marriage, but I now know that occasional heartaches, compromise and love go hand in hand. Happiness on that front is also possible when you strengthen your connection to the infinite source of all love, and learn how to maintain that presence within yourself. Then you are fully capable of being in a successful, long-term loving relationship. I have found that over time and with practice you can feel the love that comes from above unconditionally, by default. It begins to spontaneously manifest daily without any effort on your part. It can be there when you awake in the morning, just because you have become attuned. I knew when this started happening to me, that I was truly ready to start helping others with the hands-on healing work. I am certain the same can happen for you, if that's what you would like to do. Helping others puts you directly in line, and when I started doing this work full-time the energy doors swung wide open, and the healing work really began.

Chapter 9:

The mind

One of the mistakes we make as human beings is thinking that the busier we are, the more we are achieving. Well, that all depends on what you think achievement actually looks like. A rat can be extremely busy running around in a wheel and yet achieve absolutely nothing.

We can be so 'immediately busy' that we can lose sight of our ultimate goal and purpose. We can have so much going on in our lives that our minds can become overloaded and stressed. After all, what is the real purpose of life? There are many philosophical ideas about this topic. I would like to suggest that the purpose of life is simple: to learn how to successfully exist, and co-exist, as spiritual beings in physical human bodies, and to learn everything that goes along with integrating the physical, mental and spiritual parts of ourselves. Everything else in life is probably superfluous to that single purpose. It's all about learning to integrate body, mind and spirit. They say 'life's not a dress rehearsal' but perhaps life is in fact, a body, mind and spirit test, or practice run.

You will see in the diagram on the following page how the spirit is at our very centre (sometimes called our heart), which is from where the endless reservoir of unconditional healing energy pours out. Previously we have talked about the healing energy travelling vertically from the top down, and yes, it does that also. Healing energy naturally flows in two major directions, from the top down, and from inner to outer. You can experience energy moving in both these directions as you practise these methods I'm sharing with you.

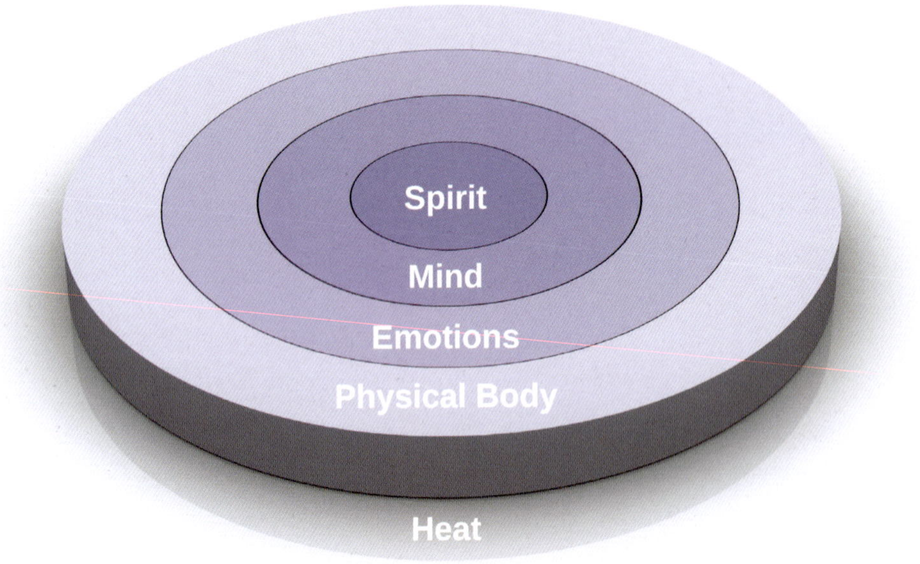

Because healing energy comes from the realm of what we commonly call 'the spirit' and we ultimately need it to reach our emotional body, it will need to pass through our mind first. However, no matter how hard we try, it's usually a diluted version of healing energy that gets through to the body, so we need to cleanse the layers of this filter, and realign ourselves regularly — especially the mind.

Let's start by talking about how the mind can be used as a powerful tool in energy healing. I will describe a simple alignment process for you to experiment with. Remember when we talked about energy exchange, and how we need to rise above our emotions in order to have any control over them? This is where the mind comes in. If we are engaged in worldly pursuits like study, work, business or pleasure, and involving our mind in these a lot, then it can become mentally and emotionally stressful. The trick is to continually reconnect to our inner, higher, pure energy source for healing. Worldly goals are great, but our health always needs to be our top priority.

Here are three simple steps you can use to empower your mind to manage your emotional state and align it with the healing energy source.

Step 1: **Identifying priorities**

Have you ever tried to completely stop thinking? It's almost impossible, isn't it? Our mind is constantly occupied with the future and the past, not to mention the present. When you combine these you have a continuous stream of thought processes going on. Most of these thoughts revolve around our ego, the desires of our body, and dealing with inevitable emotional stress and pain. Very few of these thoughts have anything to do with our higher purpose, the ultimate truth, or unconditional love and healing, and therefore they simply distract and disconnect us from the pure source of universal truth, light and healing energy.

Here are some of the distractions I am talking about:

- focusing on a promotion at work
- personal business success
- the new house or home improvements
- the perfect spouse or relationship
- new car, boat, or a holiday
- the perfect body and sexual gratification
- the latest technological gadgets
- sporting achievements or other accolades
- food gratification, addictive substances
- status, power and position
- more money in the bank.

I urge you to be brutally honest and to openly test yourself with a 'reality check'. Take another, slower look at the list above. Then sit down and try to quieten your mind and see what thoughts pop to the surface. I guarantee, for most of us, 99 per cent of these thoughts will have something to do with that list. One way you can gauge your priorities is by what is 'front of mind for you'.

You've heard the saying 'Put the cart before the horse'. Let's apply that principle here, and experiment by changing that list to a new list of higher priorities. Try meditating again while directing your focus on these things instead, and see how it feels. Think about:

- your higher purpose
- spiritual progress
- inner peace
- love
- lasting happiness
- physical health
- truth and light.

Turning your focus to these things initiates the process of connecting with healing energy within yourself, as it emulates your higher perspective, centres the mind, and quiets many of the processes around past, present and future worldly endeavours. To start with, it's good to just practice focusing your thoughts on these higher priorities during the day and see how you feel as a result.

The first list encompasses what you would call 'worldly endeavours'. They serve to do nothing more than distract us from our true purpose in life, which is to learn about ourselves, understand our body, our mind, and integrate these with our pure, loving spirit. We then become a body/mind/spirit being who is patient, kind, tolerant and compassionate with others. Ultimately everything else will fall into place once we have a clear connection with this cosmic blueprint that was laid down by the great universal intelligence, and conveyed by unconditional healing energy. We connect with our built-in higher guidance mechanisms. Everything then becomes less painful and difficult, and our path is made clear. Confusion becomes a thing of the past and we know exactly what it is we need to do next. Worldly endeavours then begin to simply manifest as natural outcomes of the creative energy we radiate. All we have done is put the horse before the cart and progress is made by default.

Step 2: **Real intent**

In the previous chapter, we talked about channelling, and clearing the channels from the bottom up. This means starting with cleansing the body, which can be done by detoxing with herbs and diet, along with some short periods of fasting when possible. We have also suggested grounding yourself, with massage, exercise, sexual activity and connecting with nature.

Next, we talked about clearing the emotional level by letting emotions out, such as singing, dancing, laughing, crying, even yelling; but most of all just being open with our emotions and letting them flow. This opens the channel for our mind to release energy, and as you do this you will be more able to take control of the emotional and physical body. You will now be moving into a place where the power of your mind is becoming clearly evident.

Now is the time to choose your thoughts deliberately in order to tune in to, resonate and connect with healing energy. Because you have opened the channels and placed yourself in the right space, with the higher universal perspective, your mind is now becoming the driver of your emotional/physical body.

Using the principle of simplicity and understanding the nature of tapping in and channelling, you can now switch on the flow of healing energy directly with the power of your mind. All you need to do is intentionally focus on a higher truth that directly aligns, tunes in, and resonates with your higher purpose and the source of unconditional healing energy.

Remember the listening, looking, feeling method of meditation and how that can give you direct awareness of the healing energy by way of light, sound and feelings. As you start to connect with healing energy mentally, you probably will get feelings in your head and brain. This can vary greatly, but generally a combination of buzzing, tingling, pressure and little electrical impulses, resulting in blissful sensations. You may get shudders, little shocks, or even strange warm magnetic feelings around and within your head and body. These are all signs that you are connecting to the healing energy. They are all okay.

The most important thing to remember is not to judge or try to process these feelings. Just let yourself feel them, let them release, and allow them to be passively processed by the healing energy. Remember the energy has universal intelligence built in. It is simply going to break down any resistance without any effort on your part. But this letting go process can take time and practice.

You just need to focus your intention towards opening yourself up and allowing this energy to travel downwards in your body and outwards as heat. When you're breathing, remember to visualise your breath going all the way down into your body and exhaling all the way from deep down, even from your feet. This generates electrical thought impulses and helps your body to release stored stress energy and toxins. Deep breathing is so healing for your body that it should become an integral part of the healing process on all levels.

Your 'real intent' should be focused towards tangibly receiving the healing energy within your mind, as both thoughts and feelings. The funny thing is, the less you do, the more you will receive. Simple meditative breathing with an open awareness will usually do the job.

Think about it: the first thing we want to do when we're unwell is sleep. That's because the body needs to stop and take a break in order to heal. We also know that if we don't take a day off each week, and a decent holiday each year, we will either collapse in a heap or get sick. This same rule of simplicity applies to our health on all levels. When we stop, take a break and do nothing, our body automatically connects to a deeper level of energy and healing. We also need to apply this basic principle of healing to our minds. After all, all sickness ultimately comes back to our minds in some way. If we could only stop our minds and put them on holiday, we would all experience a much deeper connection to unconditional healing energy.

It's not really possible to completely stop the human mind, as you will have experienced. Even when we sleep our minds keep racing around with all kinds of strange and obscure thoughts. Here is one simple, effective way of calming the mind.

Step 3: **Focused thought**

Because it's virtually impossible to stop the human mind from thinking, the best approach is to use focused thought. This is a very common practice throughout the world in various religions and spiritual practices. For example, prayers are recited in chapels, and mantras are used in meditation. The key thing is to keep it simple.

I have found over many years of practice that the most powerful words to use in meditation are 'I am'. The reason for this is that nothing goes deeper. It connects with your very identity, your ego, and your spirit. Think about it — probably the first sentence you uttered was 'I'm hungry, Mum'. If you repeat the words 'I am satisfied' enough times, you will quickly find that your hunger reduces. A great weight loss technique by the way.

However, I suggest choosing something that you already know you need to work on mentally. If you don't know what that might be, start with something that is causing you stress. For example, if you are the kind of person who gets easily financially stressed and worries about money a lot, you could choose to focus on a short phrase like 'I am abundant'. If you are the type of person who feels isolated from others and the world around you and is lonely, you could choose to focus on a short phrase like 'I am connected' or 'I am loved'.

There are literally endless possibilities when it comes to beginning this process of focused thought. What I am going to share with you below, however, is a list of phrases you can use to tune in to healing energy and which trigger the most powerful experiences of energy movement.

I suggest meditating as previously outlined, with the 'look, listen and feel' technique, for a few minutes each, while slowly repeating these absolute truths in your mind. As you repeat these phrases you will get confirmation of their truth by way of direct experiences of healing energy. Feelings of peace, love, warmth and the release of pain, stress and grief. The phrases will help resolve false, negative beliefs, attitudes, or opinions and directly increase access to healing energy, by clearing the filtering mechanism of your mind.

It is good to repeat them slowly and breathe deeply as you ponder each one. Try using one phrase per week, as this will allow time for them to integrate and manifest their full healing power in your body, and radiate into your life in general. You will naturally want to race through them for quicker results, but trust me, the more time you spend on each one, the deeper your results and your healing experiences will be.

There are 46 weeks of healing meditations below. If you can do 10–20 minutes of meditation each day you should achieve rapid and measurable healing. If you can do an hour or more, you could also have massive enlightenment experiences similar to those I have described. There is no limit.

You can read this list quickly through now, but you will want to come back to it later and work through the individual phrases over the coming weeks, months, and in some cases, years. The fact is, you will never stop benefiting from this practice.

'I am' healing phrases

I am a spirt; I am in a body; I am open; I am worthy to receive; I am inspired; I am patient; I am trusting; I am looked after; I am beautiful; I am pure; I am light; I am energy; I am spiritual; I am a channel; I am connected; I am eternal; I am accepting; I am making progress; I am nourished; I am precious; I am loved; I am fulfilled; I am content; I am joy; I am compassionate; I am tolerant; I am forgiving; I am impartial; I am detached; I am peaceful; I am giving; I am loving; I am growing; I am learning; I am changing; I am healing; I am one with everything; I am receiving light; I am receiving knowledge; I am guided; I am truth; I am a creator; I am unconditional; I am love; I am that I am; I am, God is, love.

For these phrases to take root and connect us to healing energy, it is crucial to remember the greater purpose of our lives. We are all here on earth to learn and make progress. We are experiencing these physical bodies and this physical world with all of our limitations. It is an integration experience. We are learning to integrate our spirit with our body, to integrate the infinite and eternal within this finite, temporary realm of dense matter. This can be frustrating and painful, and because of this, many false ideas about life spring into being.

For us to fully integrate, we are challenged with these false ideas from all directions, and loving, tolerant relationships should become a priority. You will notice in the list of phrases that many of them revolve around patience, kindness, understanding and forgiveness. This is because we simply can't integrate within ourselves without also harmonising with other human beings. Love is absolutely central to the entire experience.

I should also mention that when using these on yourself you will sometimes experience resistance to them. Your mind will disagree and argue against some of these phrases, and that's perfectly normal. Remember we are here to learn. If we already knew everything there was to know about experiencing this type of existence then why are we here?

Dropping our ego and humbly letting go of our past ideas can be difficult, but ultimately it leads to the most happiness and healing. If you find yourself mentally arguing with any of the phrases then take it as an encouraging sign, and take a little more time with it. This means you can make some rapid progress by taking that particular phrase on board in more of your meditations.

Choosing your phrases

The fact that you may not agree with some of the phrases means you have work to do, and a mildly contentious phrase could be one worth starting with. For example, 'I am worthy to receive' is challenging for many; or 'I am loved' may not ring true for some. Some phrases you will quickly accept and the feeling of healing energy will confirm their truth. Those which you find a little harder to accept will require more time and meditation, but the energy experiences can be even more profound when they are accepted. This is where the most healing can be found. Working with the phrases you find the most challenging will bring you the deepest emotional, and the quickest physical, healing.

You will be able to recognise acceptance of the phrase immediately, by the sights, sounds and feelings that come within just a few short minutes spent meditating on the phrase. Once you start fully accepting the phrase the energy will make itself known to you and peace will come. Eventually, the phrase will become absolute knowledge and the energy will take over, healing will flow, and a soft warm light will appear to shine within you.

Of course, there are almost endless combinations of words you can use, and these can be tailored to your individual needs. I have chosen to use these phrases based on my experience, and after seeing thousands of patients in my clinic. These are the most commonly applicable phrases.

How the phrases heal

I've used 46 phrases because within every cell in our body we have 46 chromosomes. Chromosomes contain our DNA, and each chromosome is responsible for a number of developmental characteristics and for healthy cell replication.[1]

At the end of chromosomes are structures called telomeres. These telomeres are like tiny DNA antennae communicating between the DNA and the body. Their job is to convey the message 'this chromosome has healthy DNA and is okay to keep replicating'. Telomeres are called 'noncoding DNA' because, instead of genetic code, they contain sequences that act as regulatory elements, determining when and where genes are turned on and off.[2]

If the telomeres on the end of the chromosome become damaged, their communication becomes hampered, eventually indicating that the cell should stop being reproduced. As a consequence, those cells cease replication and die off. Cancer cells, on the other hand, have intact telomeres and trick the body by lying about what they are. They must have been defying the truth or receiving and believing false information somehow, which poses an interesting question. Does false information such as instilled beliefs, attitudes and opinions contribute to 'imposter' cell formation, and can the truth prevent this from happening? I'll leave that for you to think about.

In normal cells, telomeres shorten with age and can serve as an early predictor of the onset of several diseases, including high blood pressure, atherosclerosis, type-2 diabetes, cardiovascular disease and dementia. Studies have shown that people who meditate using positive phrases maintain increased telomere length. Essentially, this means the cell's DNA is staying more intact by meditating. Interestingly, the mechanism behind this anomaly is not yet fully understood.[3] That's a fascinating discovery, don't you think? Let's imagine for a moment that as you meditate and repeat the healing/truth phrases, you are tuning in and receiving informational energy directly from universal intelligence that is communicating with your cellular DNA via telomeres, overriding any false signals that may have been previously sent to those particular cells in your body.

Even more interesting, from a psychological perspective, telomere

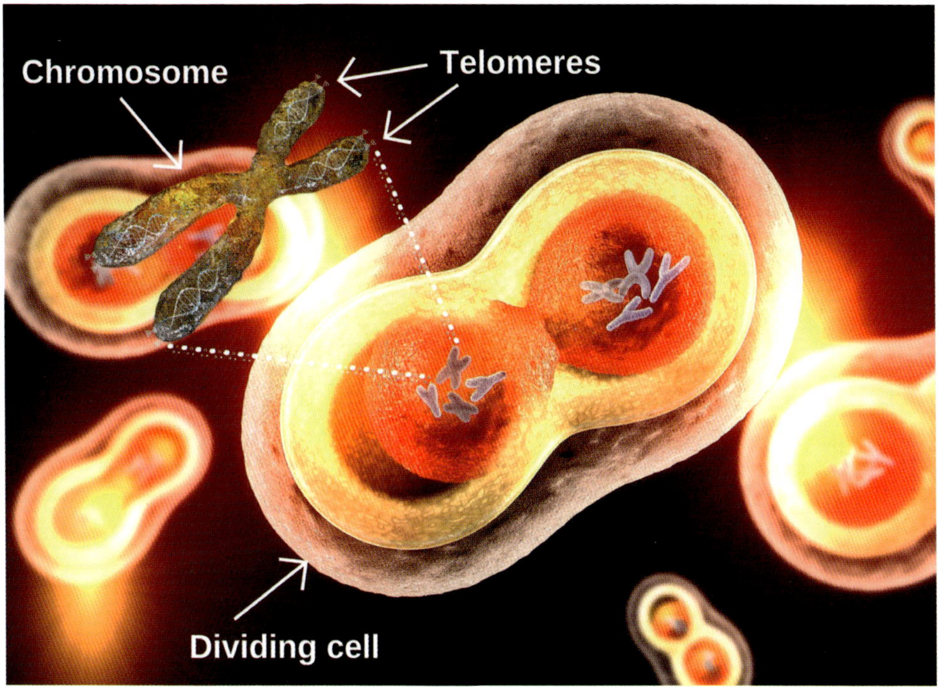

shortening can be accelerated by several behavioural elements, including a bad diet, lack of sleep, smoking, alcohol abuse and a sedentary lifestyle. It's therefore no surprise that several psychological factors, such as personality characteristics, psychiatric disorders and mental stress, are also known to affect telomere length. Once again this points to the theory that accepting absolute universal truth can protect and heal our DNA.[4]

As you meditate and repeat the healing phrases over time, your body will receive its full pattern of information, and wayward cells should begin to function correctly again. You will feel the stress energy change to peace, gentle warmth and bliss in your body, and this indicates cellular healing is taking place.

Anyway, back to the phrases for a moment. To achieve my highest energy experiences, visions, and so on, I have often used the last phrase, 'I am, God is, love'. This phrase is last because it's what I consider the most profound, so don't rush into it. Let me explain how I do this in more detail.

Let's start with the first two words. When you say 'I am', it immediately calls out to your ego/identity, which is exactly what we talked about rising above and letting go of. So, when you think the words 'I am', it is good to think of that higher perspective, your spiritual centre or heart within yourself, which is the place from where you can feel true unconditional love, and also the place where the healing energy actually enters the body and emanates from. The key is to get your heart and mind to synchronise and harmonise with the healing energy and leave your ego out of the picture. I suggest mentally repeating these words very slowly; in fact, it's good to just say 'I am' on a slow inward breath.

The next two words 'God is' are referring to the great, infinite, intelligent source of life and the universe, which also includes the healing energy. Depending on your belief system or religion you may replace the word God with whatever fits into your thought system or spiritual understanding. The point is this: when you use the two words 'God is' after the two words 'I am' you are essentially acknowledging the existence of your spirit, and the great universal spirit, and connecting the two. I suggest repeating the two words 'God is' slowly, on a long outward breath.

Lastly, you can mentally repeat the word 'love' in the next deep breath. Now you have the connecting mechanism that is responsible for giving us all the light, knowledge and information that our body needs to heal itself and to be made whole. Fully understanding this unconditional, infinite, living and breathing love energy that comes from the universal divine source will probably take many lifetimes' worth of learning, both in this physical world and into the next. But contemplating it and focusing our thoughts on understanding the connection between that 'I am' within us and the great infinite intelligence behind and within our universe will bring us the strongest connection to unconditional love and healing energy possible.

I can't stress enough the power of practising your healing

meditations on this and the other phrases. Searching with your looking, listening and feeling senses while breathing slowly and repeating these phrases can bring you deep, quick and powerful healing results.

Getting results

Okay, now you have made the connection, opened the channels and intentionally encouraged the healing energy to flow, you should start seeing some results almost immediately.

The reason is that you have now gone directly to the source, you know what you're looking for, what it might feel like, and how to generate energy movement. If there are blockages or resistance within your body or mind, they will show themselves as pressure, pain, shuddering or electrical and magnetic tingling. Remember, the healing energy requires nothing of us other than to tune in and let go, so there is nothing to fear. All energy movement is positive.

Time out, space and relaxation will be very important in allowing the results to manifest. It may take some time and practice, but it's not something you can force. A sure sign that you are getting results will be a sense of lightness, peace, and warmth coming from within your body and radiating outwards. Another good sign is energy moving down through your body, so you may experience more physical energy in your lower body.

In the next chapter I'm going to talk about a specific method to use your hands and encourage more energy to move and more healing to take place.

Keep up the good work.

My story continues . . .

As my own personal healing continued, it meant changes in my life. I started to look at my long-term diet in a different light and was determined to kick any other bad habits — which, incidentally, took some time. I found a house where my family could live, plus it had a semi-attached dwelling that I could use as a herbal healing clinic. I had also completed my first Diploma in Herbal Studies and was ready to start seeing clients professionally. We had decided to live in a small town temporarily, near family, so there was really no competition in my niche market. The word spread fast and before long people were regularly appearing at my door. I will relate a couple of cases of healing that I know could have happened no other way, except with this energy healing method I had developed. In those days I didn't have a massage table for people to lie down on, so it was just sitting in a simple chair, like a dining-room chair. I would lay hands on their head, shoulders and front and back of the stomach area. A session would take around 20–30 minutes. This sitting method was something I had seen used by spiritual healers in my explorations, and it seemed to have merit. I remember many cases, but I will relay just three that particularly stand out.

Case 1: The first case was a woman in her late twenties. She appeared to be in good health, apart from the fact that she and her husband were failing to conceive a child. She said they had been trying for nine years and had done everything the doctor could recommend. I suggested some cleansing herbs, and proceeded with the healing. At first, everything was normal and peaceful, until I placed my hands either side of her abdomen, one just below the navel and one on the lumbar spine area.

There was immense magnetic energy pushing against my hands but I kept them firmly in place. Heat started to radiate from her body and I knew this was a very good sign. Energy blockages/ complexities produce heat (as they create resistance) and this heat eventually dissipates as the complexities are broken down. The heat from her body was tremendous and she felt it strongly, commenting on it after the session. You could liken it to putting your hands about 40–50 centimetres away from a fireplace: it was the most heat I have ever experienced during a healing session, to this day. After the healing I said to her, 'Okay, now I want to you to go home, and tonight, do what you need to do with your husband', and she laughed out loud. Exactly eight weeks later she appeared at my clinic with the news: they had conceived a baby, and she was precisely eight weeks pregnant. We both knew how this had happened and were both equally blown away by the result.

Case 2: In the small town we were living in I had been attending a local church, where we could go and sing songs and enjoy meeting the locals. At this time I was still investigating different faiths to see if I could find similitudes or deeper truths that fitted in with my experiences. It wasn't quite working out with this group, as I had already had some direct experiences that contradicted the judgements they were placing on other faiths or other religions. I was open to all religions being good, and true to varying extents — a piece of knowledge that I still hold today. During this time, members of the church had heard about my practice of healing and were also saying that I was dealing with the Devil. This was pretty much the last straw for me when it came to that type of overly judgemental Christianity, and I stopped participating with that particular denomination.

One day a leading member in the community turned up at my clinic asking for help. She had a large mole on her eyelid that had been growing slowly over several years, and was not going away. The doctor had said she could completely lose the eyelid if they operated on it. This was an interesting case. I did not lay hands on her, as they were not comfortable with that practice. The woman's husband said that if I was working with God then he would perform the healing. This was a matter of faith. I knew that with enough faith, healing energy could still be passed on to this woman, so I proceeded to offer her a verbal blessing. It must have been a combination of my presence, along with her faith and the healing energy transferred within the room that did it. Again, after a couple of weeks had passed they returned together. The husband reported to me that after only a few days, the mole had just fallen off. I later heard that they had left that church because of the harsh judgements made about the healing work I was doing. I am still a Christian today, but I know for certain that not all churches are 100 per cent correct with what they teach, especially when it comes to their sweeping ideas about judging others to be evil.

Case 3: A lady in her eighties would come in every 2–3 weeks for a healing on her bad hip. She would come in on crutches, receive an intense amount of heat in the affected hip and leave walking without crutches. She was exclaiming 'it's a miracle' each time. Unfortunately, she later found out that her hip joint had almost dissolved completely and had to be replaced. What struck me was her ability to get up and walk after each healing session. Pain is one thing that can get immediate relief with this technique. Remember, there are almost no limits to what can be done, as the realm of energy fields underlie the physical world. We are energy first, then we manifest in the physical.

Chapter 10:

Using your hands

If you've read this far you'll have noticed that we've really gone into the background around what the energy is, how to connect with it, the nature of healing energy, how it moves, and so on.

It's really not complex, and ultimately, simplicity is the golden key to getting this technique to work. When you strip it down to the basic principles, it couldn't be any easier. Instead of choosing to repeat old patterns we simply choose to meditate on accepting new patterns. This does not require any effort; it's simply a choice. It's not hard work, but rather a decision to let go.

You don't need to do a lengthy course of training, gain a degree or anything like that. A certain percentage of us have a bit of a healing gift. It's an innate ability that we're born with, like an artist or a musician is born with a certain something. Others may need to work at it a little bit, but in essence, it's a very, very simple thing to learn.

Think about this, for example. When you get a headache or pain in your body, your natural instinct is to place your hand there to comfort yourself. We think of this as just a natural instinct, and it is. Humans have a built-in healing touch, and we all have it, without exception. That's because our hands have the ability to transmit this healing energy outwards from our hearts.

Think of it another way. When a baby cries and you pick up the baby, your natural instinct is to rub the baby on the back and use your hands to comfort it, plus your heart opens and you feel a sense of compassion, empathy and love. So, there's more than just a physical thing taking place with the hands. There's actually an emotional, mental and spiritual thing taking place there, and it's called energy healing.

The transfer of this healing energy is manifesting because compassion is a form of love. It's caring about another person, and that's immediately going to switch on the inbuilt healing power that we have with our hands. When we do it with ourselves we're actually showing ourselves compassion, whether we're aware of it or not. That can sometimes be the hardest thing for us to learn to do — to have self-compassion, self-love.

I want to talk a little bit more about the energy now. We've already spoken about this previously, but the healing energy is a form of energy that's real and tangible.

Healing energy is measurable by our own senses and comprehensible by human consciousness, and just like the other five senses, our sixth sense is real. It's the feeling of the living electromagnetic biofield, and there is molecular evidence that supports the mechanism by which we can sense changes in these fields. It involves the major electrolytes in the body, which open channels within cell membranes.[1]

Yes, of course, we already know we can feel it, but we can still use the method of meditation, tuning in, and resonating to become more aware of feeling this energy, taking on the same perspective as the universal source of healing energy, the unconditional source of intelligence and life. When we tune in to that, we're able to start connecting and feeling the healing energy grow clearer and stronger.

Remember how we spoke about healing energy as being a form of electromagnetism, or electromagnetic energy? That energy travels directly through our body, especially through our nervous system. Think about this for a minute. Our nervous system runs on electricity, which is, in essence, an electromagnetic energy, a form of light. Our brain and our nervous system are the channel for that electrical energy. Let me tell you this for certain, it's also the major channel through which healing energy moves. Our nervous system is our brain, our spinal cord, and our peripheral nerves, and they then branch out to connect with the muscles in our body.

We all know we can get electric shocks. We also know that electricity travels through our bodies quite well. It's the same with healing energy, but it will only travel when you connect the circuit. In other words, when you touch somebody and you show compassion with your hands, you're creating a solid connection for that energy to move through. You can, however, connect with somebody quite well just by moving within their EM biofield. You can also connect remotely, but that's more subtle and advanced, so I'm just going to focus on the hands-on method.

These connections apply to us when we want to do self-healing. Let's talk a little bit about how to heal yourself with your hands. I am going to show you the key points on your body that are most important to connect with.

As we spoke about, we need a connection to take place with the hands in order for the circuit to be complete, so that energy can flow. This energy emanates, you could say, from our heart. We've got an energy point that is above and beyond our physical brain and it's in our centre, our core, our spirit, our soul. It's where the body and the spirit meet. We often use the term heart, soul or spiritual centre — our spiritual heart — and that's actually where the energy emanates from, in the body. Although, as you know, we've spoken about it coming down, it does in effect come down through the brain and the nervous system; but this heart is another point where, at the very highest level, it disperses into our being.

The spiritual heart is where we release and share absolute compassion and love, and it's also where our spirit centre rests within the physical realm. You'll see that in different philosophies and religions it's indicated around the centre of the body, or solar plexus area, but it does vary.

When we have compassion, when we care, our spiritual heart opens up, and when we put our hands out we are opening a channel for this energy to travel through our body. It travels to our hands. What we need to do then is place our hands on a person, or on ourselves.

In this case, we're going to work on healing ourselves with our hands, looking at three main positions.

When you've got a headache, you naturally place your hands on or rub your head, but what I would recommend doing is putting two hands on your head. Often, this is easier to do when you're lying down. Use the points on either side between temples and ears, or on top of your head just above this same position, where your hands naturally fall with elbows bent. This can even sometimes be on the back of your head just above and behind your ears, using two hands. These points on the head are very powerful, and you will find the longer you spend working on your head, the clearer your looking and listening meditations will become. You may experience very powerful magnetic energy around

your head. This could take some practice to understand, so be gentle with yourself and relax.

Next, placing a hand over your heart itself is very effective. What I find excellent is to put one hand over the heart and one hand over the stomach, almost side by side.

Those points are extremely comforting and self-assuring. When you use both hands you're creating a nice, almost figure-of-eight circuit, which is fantastic. You can do these two points together: lay the hands on these two spots, do the tuning-in exercise with the meditation, and repeat in your mind the healing phrases we talked

about earlier. Then, just open yourself up to allow the energy to flow and to feel the energy move.

The most difficult thing for people sometimes is to have a sense of self-love and self-compassion. That's why it's important to lay hands on yourself, because it gives you a natural instinctive response that you're showing compassion to someone — in this case, yourself. The easiest way I find to do that is to go back to what we spoke about earlier and adjust our point of view/perspective — what I call 'taking a higher perspective'. Essentially, this is going above your own personality and ego, viewing from beyond, seeing the big picture, and realising that you're just like every other human being on the planet. We're all struggling, suffering and experiencing pain of some kind. There's anxiety, and there's stress. There's emotional turmoil. All of these things go on throughout our lives and there's no way of avoiding them. It's just a matter of how we deal with these incidents. Self-healing is a very effective way of going within, processing, releasing the stress, learning and growing from these experiences.

When we physically lay on hands and tune in to the healing energy that we've talked about earlier, we immediately start feeling peace, and stress starts to move out of our body. With your sense of feeling in your hands, it's worth noticing the electromagnetic energy movement. You may feel a kind of tension developing in your hands, which is due to the magnetic field interacting. Where there is tension or even pain, there is energy that needs to be released. Just breathe and allow whatever comes to the surface, and heat should start to radiate. The tension will then begin to dissipate. I will talk more about this process soon.

Lastly, I should also mention the torso points on either side, just below your ribcage, where your digestive organs, liver, pancreas, spleen and gall bladder reside. As part of the gut–brain feedback system within the body, these digestive organs not only have to contend with toxins but also emotional stressors, all of which affect us hormonally. Giving healing on these positions can have rapid, noticeable effects.

So those are the main hand positions that I suggest: two hands on the head, one on the heart and one on the stomach, and one on each side of the torso, around the digestive system. It's good to start from the top and work your way down, but, to be honest, it really doesn't matter. If you can do this for five or 10 minutes a day on each point, you're going to be giving yourself substantial self-healing. Even the meditation alone starts the ball rolling, but the hands-on self-healing takes things to the next level.

Now I'd like to talk about what might happen, what you might feel, and the way you can actually enhance this process.

One thing I've found is, when you're really connected with the healing

energy, your hands actually emit quite a bit of magnetism and potentially you can feel it. Some feel it more strongly than others. When you push your hands together, let your muscles relax, open up your senses, and you may just feel a gentle magnetic resistance between your hands.

You might start to feel a magnetic push or pull depending on what's going on, but generally, you'll feel a push, like opposing magnets, and you might feel some warmth start to generate between your hands. When you place your hands on the body you might feel warmth, and generally, when there's a lack of energy in your body you'll feel the hands being pulled in, and when there is excess energy your hands will be repelled. You may have met people who have a lot of baggage and stress in their lives. They tend to repel other people and eventually they push people away.

In other words, parts of your body that have been under depletion, with not enough energy, will draw you in, so your hands will literally be pulled in and energy will flow into that area. If there is stress or other build-up in the body, which is the most common thing when we have bottled-up energy, it becomes bigger, there's a mass of energy, and you'll feel it pushing your hands away. You'll need to gently push into that excess energy until you start to get vibration or heat. The healing energy will simplify and correct the complex, and eventually, that excess energy should disperse as heat, and the push will diminish.

There's definitely a combination of different things that can happen, but you don't need to over analyse it. You can't do any harm, so simply let it happen and trust your instincts.

Last, but not least, you can actually encourage this energy to move a little bit quicker by moving your hands around. You might have had your hands laid on the body for a few minutes, and you feel that there's energy that needs to come out. Sometimes there may even be pressure or pain, or discomfort as the energy moves — a bit like popping an energy pimple, or passing a stubborn, large bowel movement. This feeling can happen as the energy is moving out. It can occasionally be a little bit uncomfortable but should bring great relief after a few minutes. You can encourage the energy to move with your hands. Apply them over your body and move them up and down in sweeping motions, outward around the top of your head and downward over the body. This all helps the energy release and radiate out from your body. That's the ultimate goal of it. Feel free to go with the flow. Usually, I sweep my hands around approximately 5–10 centimetres away from the body.

There's no strict protocol you have to follow. Just allow yourself to be guided and directed by the energy and by your intuition. That's what I really love about this method: you do what you feel comfortable with. Go where the pain is. Go where there's discomfort or stress. If you go with what feels right for you, you'll get a great result.

With a little time and practice, you will develop a sensitivity to the energy and feel what is needed, by default. Just like you used to rub your sore back, or rest your aching head in your hands, you will find it becomes second nature to caress your energy field and comfort your stress points with hands-on healing.

Processing pain

One of the most difficult things to overcome when going through any holistic healing process is letting go of past hurt, trauma and emotional pain. We talked in chapter 1 about how we develop an ego structure; and our false expectations of fair energy exchange with the world in chapter 2. It's these two things that form the basis of our pain. In Buddhism, it is called attachment.

Once we start down a path of healing it's inevitable that pain from the past is going to surface. When we start applying the ultimate universal truths with our mind and showing compassion to ourselves, the healing process will escalate and these past pains will come up as visceral emotional feelings.

Before we delve into this a little further, let's take a quick step back and talk about energy again. Everything in our universe is a form of energy, either a solid, liquid, gas, subatomic particle, waveform, emotion, thought or spirit. No matter what form energy takes, it will, or has, simply moved from one form into another. This is the first law in physics, the law of conservation of energy. It's important to remember this when it comes to healing from our past.

Every event that has ever happened to you throughout your life has had an energy effect on you, whether it be uplifting or crushing. An uplifting event allows you to open yourself and release your infinite, loving, creative energy. In contrast, a crushing event, such as mental–emotional trauma, accident, financial ruin, material loss, natural disaster, lost love or illness, is much harder to process and therefore causes your energy to be entangled in a complex process.

In theory, it's all just energy moving from one form into another. The problem lies with our ego, and our expectation that only good things should happen, are acceptable to us, can be processed and let go. So-called 'bad events' leave their unacceptable energy with us. Therefore, we struggle to process them, and we often don't allow the associated energy to be assimilated and released.

The process of unconditional healing will challenge these unprocessed energies, allowing them to move and be released with almost no effort on our part. However, it's worth repeating, we do tend to hold tightly onto many of these perceived 'negative' events and use them as anchors to maintain our self-constructed ego/identity and beliefs. Letting these energy complexes go also requires us to let go of the related ego construct or belief we have built around them, and that's where we're often the most deeply challenged.

Thoughts such as, 'My family member was not meant to die'; 'That accident should never have happened'; or 'My partner should not have cheated, lied, or walked out on me', hold up our energy flow. What we need to learn is an acceptance of all things as simply energy moving from one place to another, to remain unconditional after the event, to accept the process as part of life's journey, and let it all go. We can learn and grow from these events, and in that respect, they are all blessings. I know this sounds too easy, but ultimately as you go through this energy healing process, tune in and connect, you will find everything effortlessly ends up as heat. Yes, just heat.

As you work with yourself, feelings may surface, pain may appear from nowhere, and a lot of thoughts, dreams and memories will come up for processing. What I recommend doing is practising a simple outward breathing release of all energy with the knowledge that you are simply letting infinite energy flow, and 'let it all go'. Imagine yourself breathing in energy from the infinite, unconditional reservoir of healing energy, love and acceptance, and breathing out the breakdown products of your mental, emotional metabolism, namely, heat.

Just like air is breathed in, metabolised (processed/broken down) and released, so will all the complex stress energies from your life be metabolised, broken down and released as heat. Remember, the world is not fair, and it never was. This world is full of error, man-made ideas, and is therefore misaligned with the higher laws of universal, unconditional love. We need to 'get over it', deal with it, learn from it, accept it and let it be.

We can't change the whole world, we can only change ourselves. The world of horizontal energy exchange has no equity, and never will. We must tap into the one-way vertical energy channel and pour that energy out into our creative endeavours. We are co-creators, and as we understand this secret to tapping energy and our channel becomes clear, we will see the manifestation of our healing energy all around us. Don't expect anything in return, just pour out your infinite energy, create, manifest, and love unconditionally.

One thing I have learnt after many years of healing work, is the importance of regular crying. I don't mean sobbing uncontrollably, or being a constant emotional wreck. What I find works best is what I call 'the crying breath'. In other words, as you go about your daily life, and especially during your meditation, you will often feel energy hit your emotional gut centre and this can cause tiny internal tremors or convulsions. As you become more sensitive and aware of these subtle feelings, your gut may twitch or quiver a little. Think of this as emotional channelling and see if you can tap into it. Breathe in deeply and as you breathe out, allow yourself to feel a gentle sadness, compassion for the pains of the world, yourself, your friends and family, and the struggles you have all had. Let your stomach feel a little softness, tenderness, and have a small silent cry of its own. Practising this method continuously will help you stay clear both emotionally and mentally over the long term.

Ultimate healing actually happens when we completely and continuously let our feelings go, let our hearts open, let our minds step aside, and drop all mental constraints. Once we have made this energy connection, simply 'letting go' is the key to maintaining a daily state of unconditional healing. In the next chapter, we're going to talk about how you can heal others by sharing this technique with them, and by channelling healing energy through your hands.

My story continues . . .

By the time I was 30 my clinic was going very well, and I decided it was time to expand. This inspired me to move into the city, where I had more chance of making a real difference, or so I thought. In fact, it turned out be a lot harder to make a living as a healer/herbalist in the city, as the costs of everything escalated. These were a challenging few years, but I kept my nose to the grindstone and was somehow able to stay in the healing work full-time. This is where I met my second wife and gained two more sons, making four in total. I also moved from my home clinic into main-street commercial premises. We expanded our shop and opened the doors for consultations on a more professional level. Once again, word got around fairly quickly and I ended up seeing thousands of clients during the 2000s. A couple of cases really stood out to me, and I will mention them briefly here.

Case 1: A woman booked in a consultation for me to see her nine-year-old son. He was suffering with epilepsy and even with the medication he was prescribed he was having fits sometimes twice a week. She was desperate for some help as there didn't appear to be much hope for his recovery. I simply went ahead and got him on the massage table, laid my hands on his head and let the energy do what it does. At this time in my work I was having daily experiences with overwhelming bliss and love as I worked with my clients. These feeling came from above and beyond myself, and often I felt my body was floating and completely absorbed in waves of energy as they passed through me. This work can be almost addictive by its very nature. It didn't actually seem like work at all. As I laid hands on this boy, I knew he was getting healing as there was a deep sense of connection with him and a great feeling of peace came between us. They left the session and were not seen again until about three years later. The mum just wanted to come back and let me know that her son had not experienced another seizure since that day, and it looked like his epilepsy was gone for good. It's hard to forget these wonderful cases, as they bring you real joy and make the hard times all worthwhile. By the way, I don't suggest anyone makes healing their profession like I did, not until it gets mainstream recognition. I think if you have a real gift for it, then maybe give it a go, but be prepared for some tough times along the way.

Case 2: I had one woman with migraines that had persisted for nine years without more than 2–3 days in between them. This was a case for a little herbal medicine as well, and in many cases I used herbal medicines alongside the healing. They may help a little, but it's important to remember that food, herbs, supplements and medicines are only working on the superficial, physical level, and that restoring the energy field is where the deep healing really takes place. Also supplements and medicines only work short-term, whereas an energy shift can often be permanent. But back to the migraines. This was another case of laying hands on the head, which resulted in a complete end to the migraine headaches. This level of success may not always occur as it's largely down to the openness of the person and their readiness to receive the healing. You are not responsible for the outcome, but merely providing an open channel. The client is the one who must receive the healing.

Another couple of significant cases around this time involved a man in his mid-forties with a bad back that appeared to heal itself overnight; and a chronic rash on the chest of a woman that also disappeared over night. It's these instant healings that are the most surprising, as that's not the normal response. Usually the result occurs over a period of time, so the instant cases are probably down to the receiver being at a specific turning point in their own personal journey. It's often the point when the self-centred ego has stepped aside and genuine humility is governing.

After about eight years in retail with a busy clinic and up to 30 staff members employed within our herbal manufacturing plant and my two retail shops, it all got too big for me to deal with financially, and consequently, I had to liquidate the bricks-and-mortar business side of things. Little did I know at the time, but this was a blessing in disguise. My life had become so busy with being a managing director, hiring and firing, fundraising and dealing with manufacturing contracts, that my healing work had diminished to almost nothing by 2008. This was a critical crossroads, and I have made a point of remembering the key principle I learnt from this experience. Sometimes bad things happen for a good reason and we should always look for the silver lining. From this experience I knew that I had to go back to my roots and start up my home clinic again. I re-invented my herbal detox programmes and began to sell them online, which is how I do it to this day. I was able once again to focus on the face-to-face healing work and spend personal time with the people I really care about most — my family and my clients.

It's a really wonderful thing to set up a room in your house that is devoted to meditation, healing and peace, and make it a sanctuary. The energy will build in that space and it will become a place to go when things are getting a little hectic. Once I put the word out, after a few months of rebuilding my programme, clients began to come out of the woodwork. People I haven't seen for 20 years now appear for a session. Something that has been prevalent in recent times is stress, anxiety, depression and the related gut responses, including constipation, irritable bowel syndrome, Crohn's disease, acid reflux and indigestion.

I won't go into any more specific cases at this point, but I will share the pattern I have been seeing since just after the COVID-19 pandemic lockdowns in 2020. The world has been, and will probably continue to be focused on growth, expansion, profits and power. This has been driving massive corporate enterprise to take over the world of trade and dominate our working lives. I see more and more people coming out of jobs feeling shattered and destroyed emotionally and mentally due to the demands of this model. Not only that but it's destroying relationships, homes and children as well. The moment I see these clients and they sit down and start to talk, the pattern is clear to see. We have over-complicated our lives, and this is ruining our health. We don't have time to eat properly, to meditate, or to properly look after those we love. I start to explain the principles of healing, including energy exchange and the disappointment the world brings when we look at our world horizontally, the unconditional nature of healing energy from above, tuning in, tapping in with peace and how simplifying things is so important to our health. Often these clients will start to cry with the realisation that this is all true, and nobody is really talking about it. Then I explain the power of the mind and how changing our mental focus to ultimate truths can give us a connection to healing energy and peace.

Often, when stressed clients get on the table and hands are laid on them, large amounts of gurgling begins to occur in the stomach area. This is a common sign of stress being released. They know this is happening because they often feel heat radiating from the area, and an emotional weight being lifted. Headaches and pain usually go away immediately, and digestive disturbances often settle down within a day or two. Herbal teas can be very helpful during this process as well. I have seen police, nurses, doctors, lawyers and high-powered executives — and also other healers — all get the same results. I have also seen many children recover from an inability to sleep, eat or concentrate, and severe childhood anxiety alleviated.

Usually with children it's just a matter of telling them a few ultimate truths and then placing one hand on the forehead and one on the stomach while having a friendly conversation about their lives. I tell them that they have a special power inside them, and that they can see colours inside their head that will give them powers if they look. They love this kind of thing, but also, because it's true, it works. They open up, feel comforted, the stress is relieved, and the healing energy moves. Sometimes that's all it takes. Healing with energy is not complex once you understand the true nature of things. I know I will continue to offer healing to those who ask for the rest of my life. It's so rewarding to see the results of something that has been intelligently built into our universe.

Chapter 11:

Healing yourself

Let's review the previous chapters and bring them all together into a practical method. We will cover some of the same ground again, so there will be some intentional repetition, but from a slightly different angle, with some new insights to connect the dots. This chapter should bring further clarity and create a more complete big picture.

Deep down, we all want to heal ourselves, but often we're our own worst enemy!

We can struggle to accept ourselves; we may feel inadequate, unworthy, afraid of rejection or abandonment. We yearn to be loved and accepted and yet we self-sabotage, get triggered by our past experiences, and behave in ways we wish we hadn't. We then have a tendency to hold on to guilt and regrets, further punishing ourselves.

All of these things may cause us to spiral into addictive behaviours, emotional eating, alcohol and drug use, or even self-isolation and withdrawal, limiting ourselves from achieving our life's full potential. Sadness, loneliness, anxiety and depression can result.

If you combine the total, prolonged, cumulative effect of all of the above stresses and their reactions, it starts to show as physical pain, fatigue and, eventually, an acute sickness or chronic disease state may occur. Does this picture sound familiar?

It's a pretty common pattern and you've probably seen it in your own family. In fact, just about every person that ever lived has gone through this type of scenario, no matter how rich, successful or beautiful they may appear to be. Nobody is immune to the process of dis-ease. It's important to remember that health is a state of calm, balance and harmony, or homeostasis. In other words 'health is a state of peace'. This occurs when the whole person, body, mind and spirit systems operate in harmony, or more accurately, resonate together as one entity. Whether you're living on a tropical island, a labourer working in a mine, a millionaire tycoon or a famous movie star, the same rules apply, and we all struggle to integrate them into our lives.

In this chapter, you will discover how your complete picture of health can be achieved by applying this overarching principle of peace in its fullness. Always remember the big picture!

Taking a higher perspective

In order to attune ourselves with healing energy, we need to rise above our worldly self and see things from a universal, unbiased position without the earthly boundaries of language, culture, country or religion. We can still maintain all of these, but we need to see things from the unconditional standpoint of a cosmic being that is eternal, and exists 'in this world' but not 'of this world'. We must rise above the worldly state and resonate with our higher, 'true selves' to gain access to healing energy.

What is this worldly state I speak of? It mostly revolves around our selfish ego. This ego is formed from a very young age and can be easily recognised by selfish or defensive behaviour. This ego is largely the result of our desires for everything to go 'our way'.

We wrongly feel at a very young age that the world owes us a favour, that everything should be plain sailing, that we already know everything, and nothing needs to be learned. However, we quickly get knocked back, and this is when our ego kicks in. They call it the 'terrible twos' when we start defiantly saying NO to our parents. Yes, it all starts from there, and many of us construct massive ego defence systems as children, teenagers and young adults, to the point where the ego takes over during times of stress and we turn back to the selfish 'false I am' ego: we say 'I am right' and 'you are wrong', 'I am qualified' in this or that field of knowledge, 'I am entitled to . . .', 'I am from this town', 'I am black or white' and 'I am from this country' . . . the list is endless. And ultimately these ego-based types of 'I am' statements are false, and not who we are at all.

We are actually an eternal cosmic being that is not from this world at all but from a far, far higher, and much different dimension where these worldly constructs serve no purpose. It is back to this other dimension we will return after our short stint on earth is over. We need to remember that, first and foremost. This universal knowledge puts us in the right place to start the healing journey.

Many people have an epiphany at some point in life that reminds them of this — a near-death experience, accident, illness or the loss of a loved one. Others may simply begin a search for truth and discover this along their journey. Either way, it's essential to drop the act and realise our eternal nature in order to progress.

All human beings are our brothers and sisters, as we are all created as inhabitants of this same planet, and all have our origins in the same melting pot of created spirits. With this knowledge we must love each other with compassion and understanding and forgive all mistakes. This is not to say we should be exempt from law or justice, but accepting this loving relationship with all human beings places you in the right headspace to be healed. This is the first step to experiencing the principle of peace in its fullness. I repeat, always remember the big picture!

Energy exchange

The energy that builds our false ego can be blamed on a deceptive, horizontal energy exchange with the world around us, which comes in the form of 'give and take', which in fact is more often than not 'take

and take'. Because of our worldly nature and our selfish egos, we tend to want to accumulate more, taking whatever we can for ourselves. We have also often developed a tendency to believe that the world owes us a favour, because of the commonly held beliefs in some type of equilibrium. Ideas like karma, yin and yang, or 'as ye give, so shall ye receive' don't actually work in this physical world. All manner of these beliefs fail and disappoint us on earth.

The nature of healing energy, on the other hand, is infinite and flows one way unceasingly. It comes from the universal reservoir of unconditional energy, similar to the energy that powers the sun, the galaxy, and in likeness to what the religions collectively call God, the creator, or the source of all existence. This energy is never-ending and has no conditions, other than resonance. We simply need to tune in and resonate to receive this energy. The simplest way to do that is with the absolute universal truth, which lies above and beyond all man-made versions of the truth.

Unfortunately, the world has fed us with so many false versions of the partial truth, disguised as absolute truth, but cloaked in another ego-serving outer shell, like a wolf in sheep's clothing. We have been told many lies by 'the system', by those we look up to: the media, our heroes in sport, cinema, music and even scientific institutions, along with many other supposedly credible sources or role models.

Parts of truth can be mixed with falsity and mistaken for the whole truth, like a cheap knock-off of a Rolex watch. These partial truths lead us astray and, just like the cheap knock-off, they disappoint us when it comes to the crunch. We find they have no real underlying substance and are missing crucial elements for reliability during the hard times. Like the cheap car, appliance or gadget, they break down and fail when we need them most.

The absolute truth was actually written into our DNA and into our spiritual hearts from day one. We all know it, deep down inside, and it's contained within the energy, the feeling and the act of what we call LOVE. This capital letter type of LOVE is not emotional, romantic or revolving around infatuation, but is the kind of love a parent has for their child. It is one-way, unconditional and infinite. This is how healing energy is received from above and beyond this world, yet simultaneously it permeates every atom of this physical world.

A parent may scold their child for doing wrong, or even punish them in some way to teach them the lesson of consequence, but they never stop loving that child. Discipline is a necessary part of love. If we don't understand the laws and principles that govern this world and the universe, and the consequences of breaking those incontrovertible laws, we will keep falling into traps, and we can't progress. Such progress is the purpose of our lives and is inevitable.

Once we understand that all things are ultimately centred within the principle of unconditional love and that all things are for our good, for our progress, and for us to learn more about the nature of this unconditional love energy, the more we learn, and the faster we heal. Acceptance of our painful trials and our tough experiences in life is key to receiving the healing energy.

Healing energy

Let's remember what this healing energy actually feels like. One thing I'm well aware of is that energy healing is seen by many as 'airy-fairy', not real, or not scientific at all, and that's why a little more current scientific evidence is worth mentioning.

Many different types of energy healing have been practised around the world in almost every culture, for thousands of years.

In recent times the scientific community has coined the collective term 'biofield therapies' for the various techniques, for which hundreds of clinical studies have been published. The vast majority of studies that have been conducted show positive results with people with cancer, arthritis, pain, anxiety and heart conditions, among others.[1]

One study with hundreds of cancer patients receiving hands-on energy healing of various modalities indicated a positive benefit for these patients in respect to pain, quality of life, fatigue, health function and mood. The healing in immune responses and cell line studies confirms that energy healing therapies bring harmony and balance to the system in the direction of health.[2]

Scientists are familiar with electromagnetic energy and its use in modern medicine including X-ray, MRI and CT scans, radiotherapy and laser treatment. We know that our body responds directly to EM energy from the environment, including visible light, infrared, ultraviolet (UV) and even microwaves.[3] High-resolution nuclear magnetic resonance has even become one of the most prized tools in the fields of organic chemistry and biochemistry.[4]

We also understand that our genes and genetic information can be changed by applying environmental energy. Thoughts, visions, emotions and even physical feelings are all relayed to and from our body, mind and brain (consciousness) via EM impulses, or waves. It would appear that almost all aspects of our biology and our planet rely on EM energy to function. Why on earth would energy healing appear to be something esoteric or mystical, when it fits well within our existing scientific framework, has clinical evidence, and makes perfect common sense?

Thousands of those who have reported out-of-body experiences during near-death experiences report a state of consciousness that is beyond the physical. Therefore it seems logical that our consciousness must somehow passively move into an 'energy field' state of existence after death. If science accepts anecdotal statistics of improvements with depression, anxiety and other mental states as proof of the therapeutic effect of drugs in clinical trials, then surely thousands of people reporting out-of-body consciousness after suffering a near-death experience would equate to scientific proof of life existing outside the physical body, and within an energy field of some kind.

In one study the vast majority of more than 1000 near-death experiencers (NDErs) surveyed rated their experiences on a scale that rated their sense of reality. Those surveyed included many physicians, scientists, attorneys and nurses. Given that over 95 per cent of NDErs considered their experiences to be 'definitely real', it would be reasonable to accept their assessment of their personal experience — and there is no good evidence or medical explanation to say otherwise.[5] Second to that is the fact that, if we can live outside our body in an energy field, then we must also have an eternal energy body of our own, during our physical lives, that is part of some great, collective, cosmic 'life energy' field.

A living, breathing, cosmic energy field, which is just beyond the perceivable field of energy for human eyes and ears, is not necessarily beyond our ability to feel with our own personal energy field. Our body's own electromagnetic energy field is well recognised. Another example is the recently developed neuroimaging technique of magnetoencephalography, which measures magnetic fields produced by the human brain, and has become one of the major non-invasive imaging modalities to study the human brain.[6]

It's just that with all of the busyness and harsh energy that comes at us throughout our lives, we slowly shut down this subtle electromagnetic awareness. As young children, many of us will have had energy experiences that we have probably forgotten. It is this awareness that we need to open up, reactivate, and expand upon in order to sense, feel and experience the unconditional healing energy. Our revision of the quickest methods to do this is coming up next.

Tuning in

As we've discussed, in order to receive energy sent from another place, the receiver must be attuned to the source transmitter. The energy of radio and television signals can be sent from the ground to satellites and around the world as electromagnetic waves at the speed of light. The light from the sun travels in the same fashion and can be received

as energy on earth by plants and by solar panels. In order to receive the energy, the receiving device must be on the same resonant frequency and be tuned in to that frequency. Think of yourself as a receiver of healing energy. Now imagine that there's a transmitter spanning the entire universe, and remember what we just covered regarding energy exchange. The energy is unconditional and infinite, it flows in our direction from above and has the nature of pure universal love. Remember the reservoir and the cosmic microwave background? It's everywhere throughout our entire universe, it flows in all directions, and it has a soft warm glow.

Let's focus a little longer on the principle of resonant transmission and reception. The antenna for a TV or radio signal must ideally match the wavelength of the signal to receive a clear sound or picture.[7] This means the antenna can pulse in tune (resonate) with the signal length and vibrate accordingly. As it does this, the signal can be decoded. It's simply vibrating in response to an energy wave that is pulsing towards it. Of course, we do this every day with light and sound, but what about the more subtle aspects of ourselves? We are receiving all kinds of energy signals from around us in the form of thoughts, emotions, intuitions, and even love.

By tuning in with the source we can receive unconditional healing energy without any effort being made. I want to highlight this point again for you here. NO EFFORT is required! The process is simply one of tuning in.

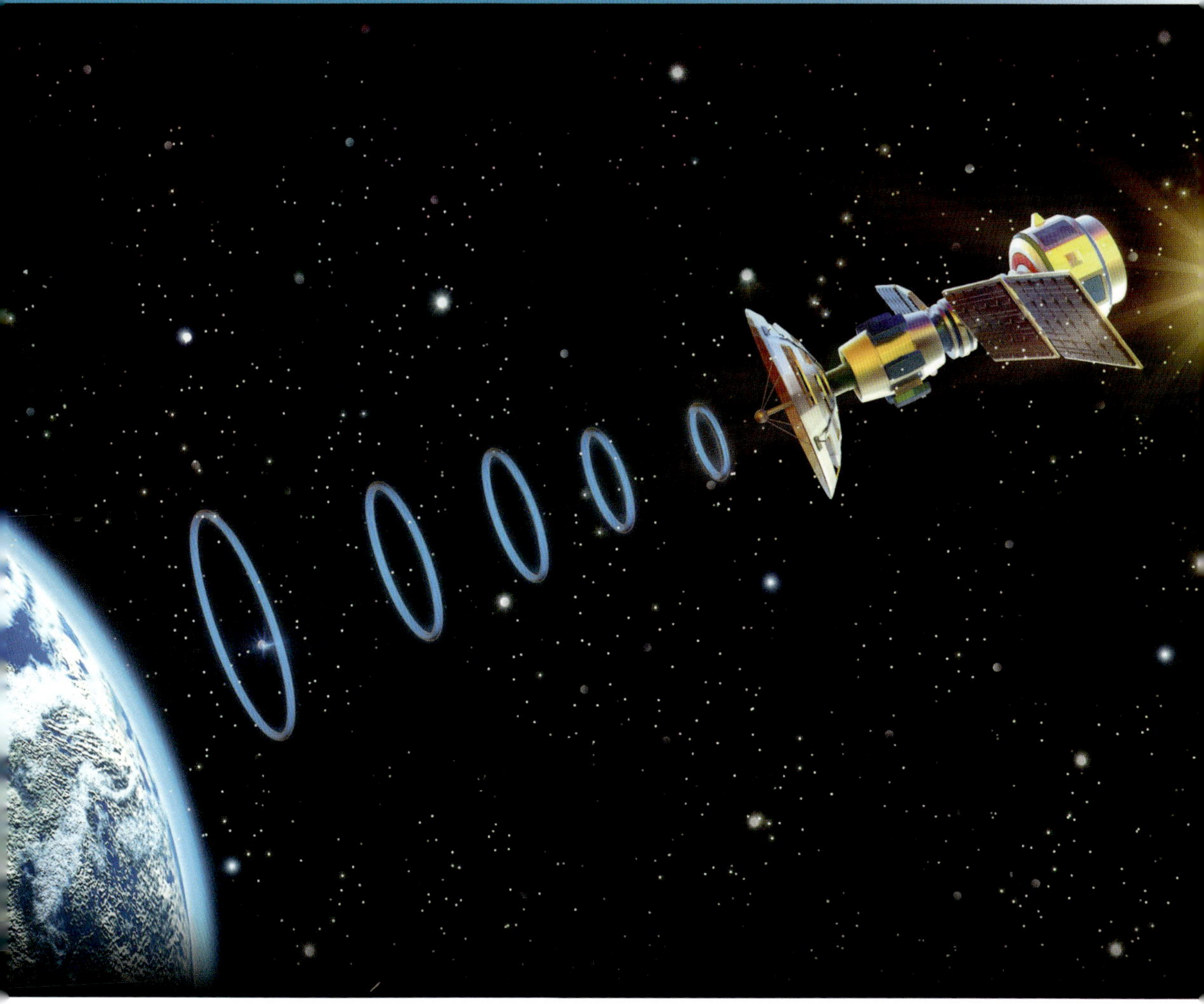

Connecting

Remember that over 95 per cent of the universe is made up of energy that scientists do not yet understand the elemental nature of. This is where our reservoir of energy is, on tap in the higher dimensional realms of existence, where universal intelligence resides. It is from this higher place where the universally intelligent, healing energy is poured out and down into the physical universe, in the form of EM/plasma information that constructs matter as atoms (in stars), bringing forth life via molecules such as DNA on earth.

That same infinite source of information and energy is creating our universe, and that's why the universe is continually expanding, just as we are from within. The jury is still out on the Big Bang theory, as many scientists still believe in the Einstein and Newton view of a universe created by intelligent design, not to mention over 84 per cent of the human race, with nearly 7 billion religious believers.[8]

The original connection within

Remember how we talked about the switch principle and how a proper connection to healing energy only takes place when we accept absolute universal truths. Because Unconditional Healing Energy is 'universal intelligence and love' and carries all absolute truths, accepting those truths is crucial to connecting to the healing energy itself. When we accept universal truth, we tangibly feel the energy increase, and when we believe something false, the energy immediately disconnects. Identifying the healing energy within us, as peace and warmth, gives us clear evidence when we have found those absolute truths.

Modern mainstream science, on the other hand, usually has no regard for our feelings when it comes to identifying truth or falsity. It's based purely on cold, hard measurable data and often makes wonderful theories to fill gaps in the data where things couldn't be measured. This is very important to remember. If something doesn't give you a warm, peaceful feeling, it's probably false, even when it may be accepted by the science of the day.

For example, there is a great worldwide debate raging between two schools of thought — 'Intelligent Design' and the Darwinian theory of 'Random Evolution'. The Darwinian and Neo-Darwinian scientific community hold to the theory that the first forms of life grew in the primordial soup by chance, through trial and error. Those on the 'Intelligent Design' side of the argument say that, yes, things may have evolved, but that they did so under the direction of a great universal intelligence.

DNA had to be almost the very first molecule of life to be formed in this universe, as DNA provides the informational blueprint of all living cells.[11] Without DNA there would be no way to reproduce a single-celled living organism, and no possibility for life on earth at all.

There are two major problems with current evolution theory.

1. Formation of DNA in the very beginning appears to be an impossible accident.
2. Evolution of DNA to include more advanced functions is supposed to be the result of random mutation.

Let's look at these problems in more depth.

Impossible accident

When you consider that just a teaspoon full of DNA can store all the written and digital information ever produced by humankind, and it virtually lasts forever, DNA as a piece of technology is truly mind-blowing.[9] It's like the ultimate flash drive, far beyond our current computer memory technology. In fact, it looks like our next wave of computer technology will be synthetic DNA-based memory storage devices.

How could such an incredibly advanced technology such as DNA be there at the very beginning of the evolutionary process completely by accident? Darwinian evolution is supposed to start simple and get more advanced as it progresses.

Random mutation

The 'mutation theory' supposes new, complex DNA code evolves from accidental or random mutations. This highly advanced code surely requires innate intelligence, or intelligent intervention, and cannot occur from random mutation.

Consider our current DNA manipulation technology such as CRISPR and our new vaccines that employ messenger RNA. We have shown that DNA has a fixed, legible sequence and works much like an advanced binary computer code which can be programmed. Clearly, intelligence can manipulate DNA and trigger the necessary changes and advancement seen in evolution.

Remember how we talked about how DNA can be altered by our thoughts? This is central to grasping the power of energy healing. Universal intelligence communicates within our very DNA and has been doing so since the beginning. It's crucial to our progress and it's certainly no accident.

With evolution theory there is an absolute disconnect between the processes of evolution and the great universal intelligence. Belief in a random, accidental model disconnects healing energy from every living thing on the planet, including ourselves.

We must be careful when teaching science in schools to not completely disconnect evolution from the possibility of an intelligent creator. If over 84 per cent of the human race believe in a creator God, such an atheistic approach can leave many of our children feeling disconnected. So many young adults feel there's no purpose to life and suffer with extreme anxiety. Showing them the possibility of an intelligent designer and an intelligent universe can show that there is a higher purpose and meaning.

When you accept that evolution is more of a controlled intelligent

Would you not agree, therefore, that something a thousand times more complex and advanced than a Dreamliner[10], namely DNA, would also be the product of a great intelligent design? The DNA within a single cell leaves the Dreamliner for dead, literally, as DNA is invisible to the naked eye, it's alive, and can multiply, accept new code directly from intelligence, transforming itself into every living creature on the planet, simply by applying a new combination of code. An intelligent creator must therefore undoubtedly exist.

process and that universal intelligence is behind the structure and function of every atom, molecule, living cell and organism on the planet, an incredible connection takes place that triggers exponentially increased access to the healing energy within. This can activate your DNA and, according to epigenetics, you can potentially download new code.

By fully accepting and integrating this profound truth, we make a massive step towards connecting to healing energy. You and I were created by an intelligence beyond our comprehension. It is the same with the purpose of our lives. Everything is intelligently designed for our learning and growth, and nothing is as it seems, or as those in the popular world around us would have us believe. This type of truth potentially resets your viewpoint and changes your reality. If not, then it should certainly confirm your belief in the existence of God or universal intelligence.

Every similar piece of absolute truth accepted, understood, and integrated into your being, activates a part of your DNA's genetic code, as it connects directly to the source of universal intelligence, truth, light and love. As you learn, grow and come to understand more of these absolute universal truths, your bandwidth connection to the healing energy expands and your signal becomes more and more complete. It's this more complete signal that creates a healthy state of mind/body.

Only truth can make the connections happen. Anything that is false cannot connect with the source of this universal love. Whenever something false, incorrect, or even misleading is accepted there is an

Any absolute truth will tangibly manifest as a connection to healing energy. In contrast, falsity is a belief in the non-existent, which can only leave you in the dark, feeling empty and disconnected.

immediate disconnect, the light is dimmed and the picture becomes clouded. It's a very fascinating, yet simple principle.

The only way to clearly identify what these 'absolute truths' are is to maintain the universal, higher perspective while seeking out a place of pure love and peace within yourself. This only comes through practice and patience. Ultimately, the healing energy will become increasingly obvious to you, and you will clearly perceive it as a witness of absolute truth.

Eventually, it can become as clear as night and day, like the lights are either switched on or switched off. There are of course thousands, maybe millions of absolute truths, and likewise, an endless supply of subtle, deceiving untruths. The tricky part is working your way through them and switching over to more truth every day. It's a lifetime's work, and most likely more work lies waiting beyond this life. Scientists say that 99 per cent of our DNA is inactive and uncoded, which leaves plenty of space for new information.[12]

The great news is, that with all that extra capacity available, you can tune in, tap in and continue to experience dizzying new heights of health and ecstasy as the great universal source of all energy, knowledge, love and creation communicates with your inner being.

Tapping in with meditation

One of the most important factors in energy healing is awareness. You have probably met people who are completely unaware of themselves and their surroundings, which can be very embarrassing for everyone involved. This lack of awareness is largely due to ego and complete self-involvement. There is simply too much going on within for the person to engage and observe things around them, and become self-aware. A recent trend in self-help circles is the practice of mindfulness. This involves living in the present moment, observing, and taking in all the beauty around us. It also means letting go of the past, dropping concern for the future, and living purely in the now. This is a great idea, but sometimes this can also be distracting, and can leave us still looking outwards for happiness.

To tap healing energy we will ideally need quiet space, enabling a tangible experience or feeling that we are connecting to something real that nourishes our soul. This can be achieved through the ancient 'observation method' of meditation that I detailed in chapter 6.

Meditation acts much like viewing the night sky from an observatory. An observatory looks into space, but to get a good view it must be well away from the city lights. Our eyes also require time to adjust, thus receiving more and more light as we look into the night sky. Meditation is the key to seeing, hearing and feeling healing energy, and realising that it's real, and it will consequently manifest to you personally.

In order to get a clear signal with our phone, television, or any device receiving information via EM waves, not only do we need to be resonating on the same frequency as the transmitter, but we also need

to be in a good location, a quiet space and have an adequate period of time to receive a clear signal. Once we get a clear signal, we start to receive all the information that was sent out by the source transmitter that we were originally meant to receive. In the same way as a television image is unscrambled by a decoder box, your DNA must get a clear signal in order to send out the right instructions to your cells, and then the organs and tissues will grow correctly and function better. The complete picture of information is then made manifest, and that makes us whole (healed).

The simplicity principle

When you consider that 'simplifying things' always makes life easier, it's no surprise the same rule applies to energy healing.

This principle can be easily understood like this. Have you ever had what they call 'one of those days'? I bet you have; we all do. It's one of those days where one thing after another goes wrong. One problem is still being worked on while yet another problem appears close behind, sometimes stacking up on you throughout the day. A day like that can quickly make you feel stressed, angry, frustrated, sad, and needing to reach for the bottle, the chocolate bar, or just plain give up. That's basically how complexity affects us. When things are over-complicated they get in the way and disrupt the state of peace we call health or homeostasis.

Remember, health is a state of peace found when the body, mind and spirit resonate together in harmony. When you simplify things, you feel better. Don't overthink it, and you will be much better off. This rule applies not only to energy healing, but also to meditation, food, medicine, relationships, work, and life in general.

Detoxing and fasting

One of the most effective ways of simplifying the energy process in your body is to go on a detox diet. It's something I highly recommend for anybody who wants to increase the speed of healing and access to healing energy. Detoxing and fasting have been practised for thousands of years and have been shown to trigger cellular renewal, retain youth, and also reset the immune functions.[13] I suggest 10–14 days on fresh produce, morning smoothies, fresh fruit and salads, veggie soups, stir-fries and curries. My book on this very subject called *Cleansed & Cured* explains how detoxing and fasting can trigger healing in your body. In a nutshell, it happens because detoxing simplifies the process of digestion and elimination, which normally require huge amounts

of metabolic energy. This allows more energy to flow into the natural processes of immune function, detoxification, healing and regeneration. What this does is create space physically, mentally and emotionally, and that's what you need to receive healing energy, and also to grow. It's that simple!

Channelling from the reservoir

One way I describe the infinite reservoir of healing energy is by referring back to the over 95 per cent 'invisible' energy portion of our universe that is still largely a mystery to science. Collectively, they call it dark energy, and dark matter, and that's because it does not emit or reflect any light. Another way to understand this infinite reservoir is to consider the elements that our universe is made from. The most common elements in our universe are the light elements (gasses) and the least common are the heavier elements (solids). You will see this represented in the illustration on page 176. The even lighter subatomic particles, waveforms, and EM energy such as heat, light and plasma are found in exponentially greater quantities.

When you allow for the >95 per cent unknown fraction of the cosmos (dark energy and dark matter), you immediately see how this chart will continue in the same fashion beyond this picture and into the realm of infinite energy. This is moving into the arena of quantum physics, which I'm not going to dive into any further because that's another deep subject. I will just sum it up like this: these finer, lighter energy components of our universe constitute the vast majority of our reality and can be influenced by our consciousness and our thoughts via the interwoven EM (electromagnetic) connection. It's within this vast energy majority portion of our universe that human thoughts and consciousness exist, above, and within which the healing energy reservoir permeates.

Even the solid matter that makes the atoms of our body are actually >99.99 per cent empty space and that's why the healing energy is easily able to penetrate us.[14] The dark energy throughout the cosmos also penetrates matter here on earth. To understand this overwhelming percentage of 'energy containing' space in our reality, consider this: if the nucleus of an atom was the size of a peanut, the outer rings of that same atom would be about the size of a baseball stadium. If we vacuumed away all this dead space inside the atoms of our body, we would each be able to fit into the tiniest particle of dust, and the entire human species would fit into the volume of a sugar cube. The rest is pure energy.

This energy, for all intents and purposes, is infinite and fills the entire cosmos. Imagine an exponential outwards and upwards expanse above the funnel chart shown on page 173 which represents mostly the table of the elements, gasses, liquids and solids. Above that, we have the remaining contents of the universe, subatomic waves, EM plasma and dark energy, i.e. 99.9999999 per cent pure energy. The beauty of this concept is that this energy is just sitting there, waiting for us to tap in.

That's why I completely oppose the Big Bang theory. Intelligent design energy flow actually works in the completely opposite direction.

Once upon a time scientists believed that the Earth was the centre of the universe and also that the Earth was flat, but now they have been able to see more. Someday science may be able to see and understand the mysterious greater than 99 per cent of existence that currently it cannot. Until then we should listen to our hearts and our feelings in order to gain knowledge of the things beyond science, and not blindly believe these interim scientific theories.

Connecting with the universal intelligence and unconditional love that are available to us will allow the energy to penetrate every atom of our bodies and fill our DNA with the complete information that it needs, removing any confusion from cellular function, immune system and healing.

Yes, you can use humility, faith and trust to receive healing energy through a healer temporarily, but only the absolute truth and knowledge can give you a permanent connection that you can achieve for yourself without any outside help, giving you real power to tap in to and use that energy on demand.

The Infinite-Creative-Expansion universe theory

Let me explain my Infinite-Creative-Expansion (ICE) theory, and you can decide for yourself what feels right. I share it because it was given to me directly, and it lines up with the rest of this energy healing method. You don't need to understand the physics of it, but it can help fit everything else into the big picture and help you better tap into the energy.

Acknowledging the potential for universal intelligent design is an important factor in triggering the healing process and, as you will see in the diagram, the infinite source material and plasma provides plenty of room for such intelligent design to work within.

Scientists know that all matter in the universe is formed by a process called aggregation, which means ‘coming together’. Pre-matter, energy and subatomic particles (waveforms), when combined, form plasma, which then fuses into atoms within stars. Those atoms are then crushed inside stars under huge pressure (fusion) to form the heavier elements. Those elements are further combined into molecules that eventually become the solid materials we see on earth by a process of transmutation. In other words, the universe is being put together/constructed from an infinite supply of invisible raw material, which must be intelligently manufactured into the expanding visible universe.

It is simply beautiful to visualise.

Yes, the universe is expanding, but the puzzling fact to scientists is that the source material (dark energy) is neither expanding nor losing its density, completely defying the laws of physics and completely destroying the Big Bang theory.[15]

According to the Big Bang theory, one tiny piece of extremely dense matter suddenly exploded and the entire universe sprang into existence. I’ve always thought this sounds a little bit silly, or to be blunt, totally ludicrous. It’s far more likely that an infinite amount of ultrafine pre-matter is slowly being condensed, connected, put together and manifesting from infinite amounts of this pre-matter source (dark matter and dark energy), as pictured opposite. It’s the ‘infinite’ part that the human mind struggles with. So let’s put that into perspective.

It has now been estimated that the universe should be at least 11.5 trillion light years across, completely outdating previous estimates of the universe at under 14 billion years in age.[16] We can currently see objects 46 billion light years away from us with telescopes, and that’s literally just the tip of the iceberg. In my eyes, this all leaves the Big Bang theory full of holes, to put it mildly. In order to truly heal ourselves, we must grasp the big picture.

Infinite Source
Dark Energy + Dark Matter + Plasma
> 99.9% of the Universe
Subatomic Particles
EM Plasma
Gasses
Liquids
Solids
Rare Metals and Gems
Solid + Liquid + Gas
< 0.1% of the Universe
Eternally Expanding Universe

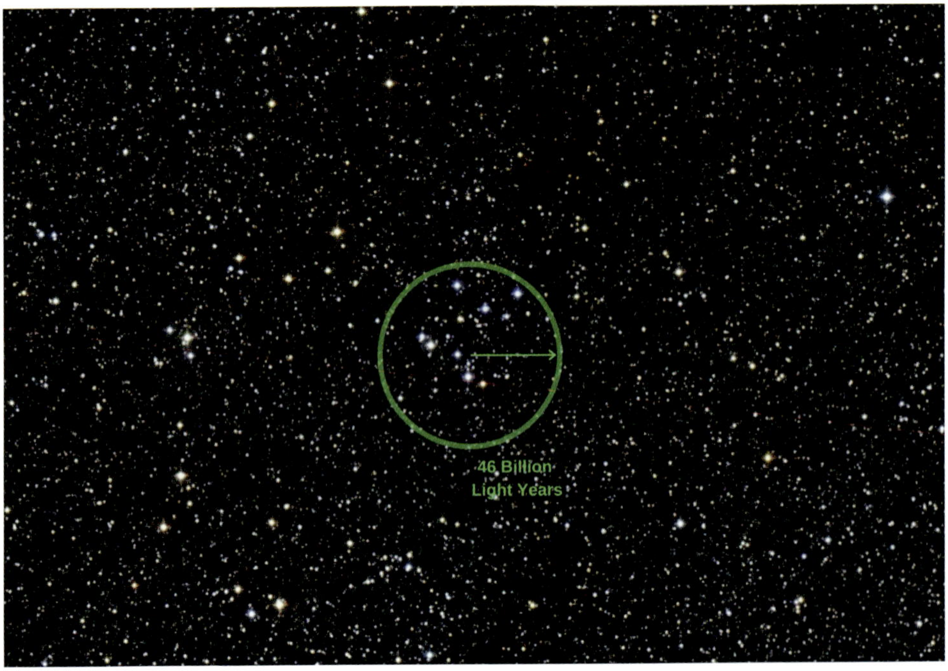

A National Science and Technology Council Committee on Science report states that:

> *Astronomers have shown that the objects in the universe from galaxies a million times smaller than ours to the largest clusters of galaxies are held together by a form of matter that is not what we are made of, and that gives off no light. This matter probably consists of one or more as-yet-undiscovered elementary particles, and aggregations of it producing the gravitational pull leading to the formation of galaxies, and large-scale structures in the universe. At the same time, these particles may be streaming through our Earth-bound laboratories.*[17]

Because this dark and mysterious 'raw material' supply is never-ending and doesn't dilute, the universe must continue to expand forever. Therefore, no Big Bang was ever necessary.

According to the laws of physics, energy will automatically flow into any space provided (diffusion) or flow into a channel from where it is drawn — that's unless there is some opposing force or pressure inhibiting the flow. The same principle applies if you continually design and manufacture something using intelligence. You will continually need more and more raw materials, so as production ramps up you will need to keep expanding your manufacturing facility. In this case, the funnel that represents the various proportions of our physical universe must push into the space around it and expand.

In the scenario I have illustrated I suggest it's actually an infinite, eternal, universal, intelligent source that's behind the scenes sending instructions via EM and plasma. The information required for the manufacture of elements, the organising of matter, the construction of new worlds, and the nature of life, are all sent via subtle EM light energy (spirit) just as all the world's major religions agree. Because of this, the universe must keep expanding eternally. Look at the way bacteria multiply, for example. Why would planets, stars and galaxies be any different? I call this the Infinite-Creative-Expansion (ICE) theory.

Human beings are contributing to this expansion, in a very minor way, by manufacturing things here on earth. Thousands of tons of space dust are landing on earth from space every year, and new layers are continuously being added to the planet's crust, including the layers we're constructing. We are all co-creators in an infinitely expanding universe.[18] We can also be co-creators of our ever-expanding selves, by connecting with infinite healing energy.

I'm sorry for throwing you in the deep end here, but a universal, higher perspective is crucial for powerfully tapping into the healing energy. Absolute healing truly involves becoming one with the universal creative force and intelligence, which you are also part of. Learning how to actively participate in the creation of your world, but also your own body, is a crucial step in your eternal progress. Understanding the one-way energy flow helps us become aligned with it, and encourages our personal energy to do the same thing: create, and expand eternally.

Tapping into unconditional healing energy is really no different from the way we draw off water, which naturally moves when you dig out a channel for it. The biggest obstacle we face when tapping into the infinite reservoir of healing energy is our 'busy nature'. We are physically, mentally and emotionally very busy creatures. This manifests as bundles of internal noise, unprocessed past or future events, emotions and thoughts, all constantly racing around within our own personal energy field. In order to tap any reservoir, a channel must be opened, and bottlenecks must be removed. Our busy internal nature does nothing but create a bottleneck, and stands in our way. We simply need to get out of our own way, and the best method of achieving that is to take control of our minds. We spoke earlier about meditation, but now we will take this one step further by including 'real intent'.

The mind

One of the great mysteries of science is the true nature of human consciousness. What exactly is it, and where precisely does it exist? Maybe it's a subtle form of internal EM plasma? We do know that impulses from the brain travel through the body as electricity and that various parts of the brain light up when we think about, or experience, certain things. This electrical power of our mind is truly incredible with how it can manipulate the physical body. Two great examples of the power of intentional use of the mind include hypnosis and the placebo effect.

Hypnosis

Studies have shown that approximately 70 per cent of individuals with chronic pain are able to experience a short-term reduction in chronic pain during a hypnosis session, and between 20 per cent and 30 per

cent achieve permanent reductions in daily pain.[19] Neurophysiological studies reveal that hypnotic analgesia has clear effects on the brain and spinal cord functioning that differ as a result of the specific hypnotic suggestions made.[20]

I always remember the night my mother went to a hypnosis meeting to learn about the power of her mind. She came home with a photo of herself almost levitating. Basically, she was balancing between two chairs like a plank with only her ankles and the back of her head supported. We have all seen people who walk on hot coals or pierce their bodies with steel rods. All testify to the incredible power your mind has over your body.

Placebo

A placebo is a fake version of a drug, or therapy, given to patients to compare against a potential new drug treatment in clinical trials. The results show that up to 35 per cent of patients given the placebo still get healing results. There are now over 5000 research articles in the world's largest medical database, PubMed, that make specific reference to the placebo effect. These include demonstrations of placebo effects for pain, depression, anxiety, insomnia, immunosuppression, ADHD and even Parkinson's disease, to name a few. Even more fascinating is that studies appear to show that fake placebo surgeries have been shown to be just as effective as real surgeries in treating coronary heart and knee problems.[21]

Conversely, when we are told to expect a negative experience, our beliefs can cause these to manifest. This is called the 'nocebo effect'. Nocebo effects have been observed in allergic disorders and severe symptoms such as nausea in cancer patients, mostly related to verbally induced and conditioned negative expectations.[22]

These two examples demonstrate the power of our mind to exert either a disease tendency or a healing influence on our bodies. But how does our mind affect our DNA?

Epigenetics

Another example of external influence affecting our health is found in the science of epigenetics. This is where a series of environmental influences have been shown to regulate gene activity. External influences and experiences can activate or inactivate genes, alter the amount of protein synthesised or expressed by a gene, and determine when a gene is expressed throughout the course of a lifetime.[23]

So how do these external energies alter our DNA?

'Make me whole' was the ancient cry to the healers of old. Our picture of health is made up of many, many pieces that constitute elements of the absolute truth. Our DNA can hold up to 3 billion potential pieces of information. It's the universal information received from the infinite intelligent source that can completely activate our DNA, and that is ultimately what heals us. That healing energy is unconditional and represents true love. When we receive that information in its fullness, we present a complete picture of health.

In order to receive this informational signal, we must have the space

Consider the television signal coming from a satellite encountering rain interference. Parts of the signal are lost and we see a messy picture on our television screen. In like manner, when we have partial truths, falsity, or external interference with our 'healing energy' signal we start to exhibit an incomplete picture of health. Isn't that exactly how we look when we are unwell? We start to present a broken picture, an incomplete manifestation of our true selves?

available. All religions have a practice of creating space by fasting, prayer, or meditation. They also create holy places of solitude such as cathedrals or temples, even using caves or mountains as places to commune with the divine. As we tune in, sit and meditate, look and listen, feel and perceive the living energy that we are receiving, we can tune in more strongly and clearly and receive a greater signal. This energy signal may contain new information, bringing us to a heightened sense of bliss, ecstasy and happiness. This will also come with a new sense of peace and contentment. This is the experience of the true state of health.

What we need to find is the time, space and place to tune in, and feed our minds with absolute truths, not worldly ideas or opinions. We need 100 per cent universal truth to see the absolute picture of who we are, and what we can become. Finding this inner peace is the ancient secret to opening the healing energy channel. Then you can start directing the healing energy intentionally with your heart, and with your hands, to get specific results.

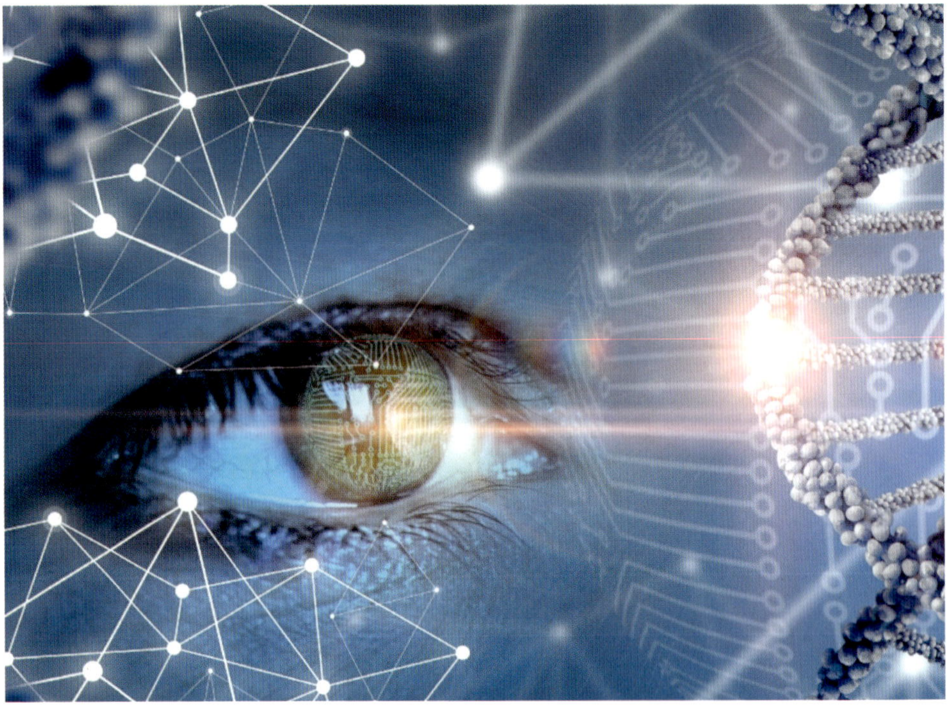

Using your hands

In chapter 10 we talked about using your hands, and a whole separate book could be written about using your hands for healing. Many systems of healing with the hands have been developed, some of which come across as quite mystical, weird, evangelistic, or just plain wacky. It need not be that way, and can actually be the most normal of practices. We tend to overthink these things when, really, self-healing is the most natural thing in the world. A simple touch of the hand can be comforting to a loved one. A stroke on the head, or rub on the shoulder, is actually an act of energy healing, so why would it be any different with yourself?

Most of us feel the tendency to rub or touch an area that is sore and tender. We need not complicate this with convoluted methods, but simply understand it like this: When you're in tune with the healing energy and express self-love or compassion towards yourself in the same way you express it towards others, the energy will begin to flow.

You don't need to understand how it flows, where it goes, or what exactly it's doing. The healing energy knows everything it needs to do the job because it's inherently intelligent. It already contains all the information necessary, without any outside persuasion.

If you have heartache, then rest your hand on your heart. If you have tension in your gut, then rest your hands there. The secret is, to practise tuning into the energy until you can feel it all around you, within you, and becoming an integral part of you. The rest will take care of itself. No need to analyse it further. Now you are ready to begin your self-healing.

I am now writing this book and realising just how far I have come on my own personal journey. I'm still learning to fully accept myself, and understand my place in the world, which is an ongoing process, as you will probably be finding yourself. This process never ends. I am realising that it's just a matter of understanding that we are on an eternal journey, and each day I need to remind myself that it's just another day of incremental progress, and to enjoy the journey. There really is no final destination, and no place of absolute endless peace. Every time I find myself in that space of unconditional healing energy, I remind myself 'this is a temporary experience'. I don't try to hold onto it, but instead, I let it go. Letting go is something I am learning to do, and it applies to every aspect of my life. I think of the phrase 'if you love something, let it go, and if it returns, it's yours' although I now use just the first part 'if you love something, let it go'. I think true love, true healing love, is a one-way thing that involves just giving without the condition of return. Yes, I do share love with my wife, but that's what really makes it work, we share by giving to each other, and that's ultimately what we all need to learn to do completely.

I'm going to end my personal story here with this thought. It is written that we should 'be as children' in order to meet our maker. Matthew 19:14 'Let the little children come to me, and do not hinder them, for the kingdom of heaven belongs to such as these.' In other words, we need to be pure and innocent and without ego in order to receive from the highest place. I now understand fully what this means. A constant state of humility, gratitude and awe as to the majesty of what I do not understand puts me in an ideal position to receive healing from above. I remind myself of this every day and sincerely hope I can remain like a child at heart. I'm looking forward to the journey ahead with hope.

Chapter 12:

Healing others

You may think that you need some special ability to heal others with energy, but that couldn't be further from the truth.

We are all born with a natural ability to give healing, and it's as close as breathing and as near as our heartbeat. From the moment your mother picks you up, she starts giving you healing, and you know instinctively that you're receiving it. That rub on the back when you're crying, that gentle stroke over your forehead when you can't sleep. Energy healing is second nature to all human beings. If you care about other people and have compassion for their suffering, then you are definitely going to find this quite natural. If you don't have that inclination then it's better to focus on yourself for now. In saying that, it's really no good trying to help others unless you have first spent time on yourself and developed a deep awareness of healing energy. If you are full of stress and pain and put your hands on others, you may potentially try and use your own energy, and inadvertently pass on your stress energy. Get yourself into the right space first, then you can move on to helping others heal.

For the giver

The paradox is that we are giving healing and yet we are not. This paradox exists for two reasons. First, healing energy is universal and comes from another dimension, therefore, in reality, it's not exactly ours to give. Second, we can't actually heal others, or force changes in other people, so we're not really capable of healing others. What we do is lovingly share truths and healing energy with them, so it's the energy itself that heals, and that only happens when the receiver tunes in, accepts, and receives the healing energy.

A baby, infant or animal can easily tune in and receive because they have very little 'ego stuff' in the way. In other words, they don't have much baggage or resistance. They are not opinionated, full of attitudes or beliefs, and are much more of an open book, so they can easily accept healing. It's the adults who usually need to make several adjustments.

Understanding the nature and characteristics of healing energy can only serve to increase your natural ability and help you to become a greater channel for it. When it comes to healing others, what you mainly need to develop is your ability to channel the healing energy, and this comes with its own special set of basic principles.

I'm now going to share the secrets I have found work best for channelling healing energy. It comes down to these seven simple principles.

1. **Tune in with the source.** Maintain the higher 'unconditional love' perspective by meditating often (daily).
2. **Become an open channel.** Keep yourself clear, physically, emotionally and mentally. You must hold onto nothing.
3. **Hold no attachment to outcomes.** You have no control over the result when it comes to healing others. Let go of any expectations.
4. **Just 'get out of the way'.** Your self must step aside as far as your personal agenda and your ego are concerned.
5. **It's not your energy.** Never try and use your own energy, but rather tune in, and tap into the infinite reservoir, using the 'I am' phrases.
6. **Love those you serve.** Remember that we are all part of the human

family and love must be 100 per cent unconditional. We are all children of one great universal family.

7. Wait to be guided. Trust the energy to guide and direct your hand movements and their timing. Don't force anything, and allow for variation.

For the receiver

It's also very important for the receiver to be in the right space to receive the healing energy for themselves. One of the most common methods used in the world is 'faith healing'. This is where the believer is healed simply because they believe they will be healed. This practice has merit because, as I said in the previous chapter, it's scientifically recognised that the placebo effect accounts for up to 35 per cent of the results in clinical trials. In other words, just because people believe they are taking a new ground-breaking medication, they get better, even when they've actually been given a complete fake, often just a sugar pill. The same principle applies to faith healing. We must allow for this as a factor when it comes to giving healing to others. Your faith in what you're doing is equally important.

If you doubt yourself, or what you're doing, or you come across at all 'airy-fairy', then it's unlikely that your subject will feel confident in what you're offering. The same applies to yourself. If you have doubts, fears or even disbelief, then it's very unlikely that you will have access to the healing energy. Remember it's the absolute truth that makes the connection take place, and doubt or fear are not absolute truths.

Preparing the mind

When I first meet a new client I take some time to get to know them and make them feel comfortable, just like we're having a friendly discussion about their family life, work, background, etc. Then I give a little background to myself and explain what the healing is all about. I explain that it's not me who does the healing and that I'm just going to help them connect directly to the healing energy for themselves.

I then proceed to share one or two of the principles of healing energy such as those we have talked about in earlier chapters. I usually draw a simple diagram and talk about the one-way nature of healing energy, coming from above, and moving down through us vertically, and how we can simply tune in and resonate in order to receive it. My other most common discussion is around the simplicity principle and how

complexity causes stress and disease. These two topics seem to work very well, as most people grasp them quickly.

I always adhere to the scientific references, keep it generic, and try not to raise any spiritual or religious eyebrows. When I talk about the unconditional nature of the source of healing energy, I often refer to the sun and sunshine as a parable. The warmth and light from the sun are one-way, unconditional, and the sun provides all life on the planet with energy. God has thousands of names, just like everything else on earth, due to cultural and linguistic differences.

It is worth briefly asking about a person's faith. That's because if you can detect that somebody has a spiritual or religious affiliation, then it can work in their favour. This is for two reasons. First, you know that they have faith in a higher power and usually that comes with a belief in healing from either universal energy or spiritual sources, and this is ideal. Second, you can often deal with them on the level of their beliefs around love, forgiveness, letting go, compassion and other universally common spiritual principles that relate to purification and self-healing.

In some cases, we talk about the meditation method, and I share the looking, listening and feeling technique. This leads nicely to the next part of the session, which is where we get specific.

Targeting the healing

Before laying hands on somebody to give healing, it's important to explain that all you're going to do is tune in to the source with them, and simply share in the process of receiving the unconditional healing energy together. The healing energy comes from the universal source and not from you, but when the two of you 'tune in' together the channel is opened up many times wider and the healing energy received is potentially much more powerful than doing it alone.

The person who is receiving the healing is the one we must target with the energy, so making the session specific to them is imperative. It can take a little digging and questioning, but what you need to look for are patterns and behaviours that may be blocking them from tuning in, resonating and receiving a good connection with the healing energy.

Here are some of the most common resistance-generating issues somebody might have.

- A complete lack of faith in anything spiritual (atheism).
- A belief that life has no purpose, and/or that life is completely unfair.
- Attitudes of anger with the system, society, some institution, or group of people.
- Resentment, unforgiveness, or bitterness towards somebody, or for past events.
- Unworthiness, a feeling of not being good enough.
- Grief or sorrow related to attachment, and a loss of possessions or relationships.

- Feelings of isolation, being disconnected, or not fitting in.
- Anxiety, fear of life situations, sickness or death.
- The big ego or the 'know-it-all'. It's impossible for a person to receive healing when they think they know everything. They will talk a lot and not listen.

None of these patterns are in line with 'absolute truth' or with the giving and receiving of unconditional love. Making some simple adjustments will greatly increase access to, and awareness of, the healing energy. It is important not to get into details, begin a counselling session, or start giving detailed advice. The key to getting a powerful experience of healing energy to the receiver is to 'keep it simple' and trigger a greater general understanding of life, or give them an epiphany around some key principle. Sometimes people may have all of the above barriers combined, so you will need to choose which is the most obvious point of resistance and address that first.

Once you have uncovered their most clear pattern of self-sabotage you can formulate an antidote. Using the phrases mentioned earlier for meditation as examples, you can come up with a short phrase that may correct some errors in thinking. I always explain that the healing phrase is a meditative affirmation. This is best described as a motto or phrase that will become their mantra for the next little while, during this upcoming phase of their healing journey. They may not accept this phrase at the present, but that's okay. You will need to explain that this is to cause a change to take place, and to resolve some conflict or resistance to the unconditional healing energy. Remember, any absolute truth will simplify their inner process and directly connect them to the healing energy.

Here are a couple of classic examples.

1. The person is angry with their ex-spouse for cheating, and consequently, they've divorced, lost their house, and are worried about future income to pay the bills. This could be making them sick, mentally, emotionally and physically. They are suffering from anxiety, depression and irritable bowel syndrome. Their healing phrase could be **'I am moving forward with love'** or **'I am trusting in my journey'**.

2. The person is drinking, smoking and suffering from addictive eating behaviours due to an abusive childhood family situation, and the resulting lack of self-esteem. This is severely interfering with their health and causing many other physical symptoms, including chest pain and indigestion. Their healing phrase could be **'I am fulfilled and peaceful'** or **'I am always loved'**.

The trick is to share the understanding that these phrases are not necessarily something they already accept or believe. Instead, the words are actually universal truths, and it's their experiences with falsity in the world around these phrases that have led them to believe in something that is not true, and this is where the disconnect took place. The new, 'true' information needs to be integrated and accepted, and it's the repetition of these healing phrases that will allow a person to reconnect with healing energy. Peace, warmth, comfort and healing will be their evidence of this truth.

They may struggle at first, but ultimately, as the phrases take hold, healing will occur, especially when practised with the new knowledge and the powerful meditation method you can share with them.

Other phrases may look like those we mentioned for healing ourselves earlier. Be careful not to complicate these phrases: keep them simple and be sure they are universal absolute truths, not just more worldly ideas. It is important that we don't use any opinions or beliefs, only generic undeniable truths.

Laying on hands

The laying on of hands for healing has been practised for thousands of years and numerous techniques have been developed. The reason it works so well is that energy is able to move very quickly when we make direct physical contact. The act of just resting your hand on somebody's head or shoulders immediately initiates the energy healing process. Once again, it's not rocket science, but more like second nature, and should be an act of loving effortlessness.

Before starting the laying on of hands, I always suggest a couple of things to prepare the receiver. I usually mention a few words like these:

- Let's meditate on the healing phrase together during the session. It will bring things up, which is natural, but when you find your mind wandering, just remember to come back to the healing phrase. This will quieten the mind.
- You can do the look, listen and feel meditation while we are doing

the healing. Take note of what you experience. Whatever you feel, whether it's heat, tingling, pressure or even the occasional twinge, it's all okay, and just part of the process.

- Close your eyes and take a couple of deep breaths and let's get started. Remember to keep breathing deep and slow.

I always start with the person lying on a massage table, but you can also do it with them sitting in a chair.

Starting from the top and working your way down is best: however, I do lay hands on the head and stomach for the first 3–4 minutes, just to establish a connection. Usually, I will spend about 5–7 minutes on each of the following four positions.

1. The head, on the temples, and then on the top of the head.
2. Next, I rest my hands on the shoulders, then the heart and stomach.
3. Either side, just below the rib cage. I never touch below the navel, but simply sweep the energy towards the feet.
4. Finally, often I will massage the feet a little, just to ground the person before bringing them back.

You can develop the exact positions and the time spent on each for yourself, based on what you feel, and how the energy is moving. If you feel the energy moving through you, that is great. It usually means that healing energy is doing its thing, and you should wait until any obvious energy movement quietens down before moving on to the next position. You may feel pressure, magnetism, heat, vibrations, small electrical impulses or even pain in your hands as energy moves and is released. You may also experience wonderful feelings of bliss and a sense of spiritual ecstasy. In any of these cases, once again, stay in that area until it calms down, and then move on. If energy is moving in any of these forms, it means healing is taking place. There is no point analysing it, as the healing energy is far too intelligent for us to understand, and all we do is complicate things, which further confuses the situation.

After you have spent 30–40 minutes on a person, the job should be done. Always suggest they continue with self-healing and daily meditations, continuing to use the phrases when they go home. Usually, I would suggest they also try the hand positions for healing themselves as well. Even 10–20 minutes a day will keep the ball rolling. Often it takes 2–3 sessions before the person is comfortable enough with the process to take it forward by themselves. Ultimately, you want them to become connected for themselves and not depend on you for ongoing healing.

The key to success in this depends on both you and the receiver tuning in to the energy together and having absolute trust in the process. Most of all, enjoy your healing experience.

Epilogue: The healing journey begins

Whether you believe in God (by any religious name), an intelligent 'universe', another form of non-religious spirituality, or even if you're an atheist, the results of using this method are guaranteed to bring healing, unless you are completely shut off to new experiences. This is because, just like you would eventually get burnt standing in the sun, you can't practise my Unconditional Energy Healing method without receiving energy, light, truth and healing. There can be no other result. Health is the default state of your body when you are aligned, and healing energy is allowed to enter. The rest is taken care of by the great intelligent designer.

Think about it this way. Albert Einstein and Isaac Newton (the two fathers of modern physics) believed there was a great intelligence behind the universe and all of their theories based on this precept proved to be true. Every waveform, subatomic particle, atom, molecule, any force, or field of energy acts in a predictable, almost pre-programmed, geometric, mathematical fashion. Even single-celled bacteria, plants, and all animals exhibit some level of intelligence.[1] It would, therefore, appear that we live in a universe that is inherently intelligent by its very nature. We could call this 'innate intelligence' and it's absolutely everywhere we look. Even a rock has some level of innate intelligence. Living things contain DNA that has the capacity to store this innate intelligence and disseminate portions of it into other less complex structures, cells and molecules. When we look out into the cosmos we see exactly the same thing continuing on forever, on a grand scale. There is no end in sight.

It is widely accepted that there exists such a thing as the 'collective consciousness' whereby groups of humans and animals share behaviours subconsciously.[2] Communication within the cells in the human body, such as the cells of the immune system, indicates that groups of single cells can also exhibit collective consciousness. If you consider how we can send out signals with our satellites, TV, and radio, which can be received globally, then it's not a giant leap to consider a well-connected universal network of consciousness and intelligence. The mechanisms for this type of communication system already exist within the fabric of our universe.

If you know how to tune in, then you should be able to receive this infinite intelligent energy, and your mind, body and DNA will all respond. Considering there are many dimensions in the universe and over 95 per cent of it is undefined by science, I think we must all be open to exploring the 'universe within' ourselves for experiential answers.

Healers throughout the ages have spoken of a great spirit, a holy ghost, and a state of peace, love, and fulfilment that comes from the absolute truth. This is felt when healing happens, and it can also seem to happen collectively. There does appear to be a universal overtone when people come together with love, which resonates within a group. Some find this group environment to be the quickest way, but it can also be a way of depending on others for an energy connection, instead of finding your own inner source. Others feel they just don't seem to fit in to these groups.

You first need to find that great healing energy within yourself before seeking out like-minded others, and then you can truly share such collective healing experiences in the most positive way. Either way, you should eventually realise that no matter where you are, you

can tune in, and the energy can be found deep within the fabric of your own being.

You may have noticed that throughout this book I have tried to keep things generic and grounded in a few basic scientific principles. I have employed this as my deliberate strategy so anybody who accepts these principles can employ this healing method.

If you look out into the universe you won't see divisions or discrimination, as those are man-made concepts. The absolute truth goes well beyond our limited partisan patterns of division. The universe is one endless symphony of cohesion and cooperation. That's what 'universe' means — 'combined into one whole'.

Whether we can see it or not, everything is one great dance of harmonious perfection. We can see nearly a trillion galaxies with our telescopes, dating back 45 billion years in every direction, and who knows what is beyond that. Maybe it never ends? Personally, I am a believer in eternal infinity, a creationist, and a healthy sceptic of both the Big Bang theory and Neo-Darwinian evolution. It's a very liberating idea, 'eternal infinity'. It's impossible to prove or disprove, but with the scientific knowledge we have accumulated to date, it's very much looking like we live in an infinite universe, with no conceivable beginning or end. I think science will eventually concede to this idea.

When you consider this timeless, endless, infinite nature of our universe, it really puts things into perspective. The beauty, perfection and harmony that exist in nature, the brilliance and complexity of our body and the molecules that it's composed of, are truly mind-boggling. We are only beginning to understand these things, including how DNA operates, how the mind affects the body, and the power we have to directly influence our genetic expression and our health. All of these mysteries are yet to fully reveal themselves as we keep searching for answers.

Science, philosophy, religion, spirituality and atheism are all different ways we, as human beings, attempt to frame all of this into some kind of coherent order. Of course, these choices and beliefs can be argued, and yet there must ultimately be underlying, absolute truths, and realities to our universe that are incontrovertible and indisputable. The true scientist is searching for these absolute and indisputable truths, and yet, coincidentally, the true spiritual seeker is on exactly the same journey. To theorise, explore, experiment and discover ultimate truths is the incentive driving both the scientist and spiritual seeker. Why not integrate these two mindsets and garner knowledge for your own personal progress and growth in the same manner?

I would say I'm a bit of a dichotomy, a sceptic with a completely open mind. In other words, I believe in endless possibilities but I don't believe anything I hear without personal research, experimentation and validation. The curious scientific mind seeks to understand by measuring data and gathering results. The spiritual seeker seeks to understand absolute truths by way of practising disciplined methods, culminating in direct experiences, to hear, see and feel within for oneself, thus building a personal testimony of said truths, and

developing deeper faith in one's methodology. Personal healing is one of those experiences that is evidence of such absolute truths. Lasting healing and peace are the fruit of true knowledge.

Ultimately, we're all made up of more than 99.999999 per cent energy and this energy is universal, infinite and somehow all connected into one great field of living energy. Scientists theorise that the universe may actually have 10 dimensions. While they are imperceptible as far as our senses are concerned, these more subtle dimensions would have governed the formation of our universe from the very beginning.[3] This is where our personal inner searching begins to closely correlate with science.

Making a connection internally to healing energy brings feelings of warmth, love and peace. Just like emotions and dreams, we can't share them fully, but we can each know they truly exist for ourselves. You can perform your own experiments with meditation by using the techniques in this book and draw your own conclusions through the direct experiences you will receive. Over time, this will become absolute personal knowledge, as your energy connections become deeper and stronger.

No matter what your beliefs or faith, I challenge you to start your healing journey afresh every day with an open mind, an open heart, a humble innocence and a keen sense of wondrous awe. These are the keys to taking your healing journey forwards. There is joy to be found in the experience of never-ending experimentation and discovery. Test the methods and techniques we have discussed and take steps each day to add more knowledge to your library of truth.

Like anything, self-healing is something that needs practice. Your body is like an instrument that you can learn to play. You can tune in, resonate and receive increasing inner light, sound and feelings as you harmonise with the great symphony of intelligent, universal life-energy. This all requires daily exercise in order to eventually become second nature. No musician can just stop practising their instrument and expect to play at full speed, let alone make progress. Your self-healing practice is no different.

I recommend at least 20 minutes of daily meditation, an hour or longer if possible. I also suggest a regular period of fasting, such as once a week. Just for a couple of meals, as this helps reset our inner connections. The other thing I highly recommend is intestinal cleansing and detoxing. I have my own programme that I usually complete twice a year, which consists of 14 days on herbs, pure fruits, smoothies, raw vegetables, vegetable soups and curries. (See my book 'Cleansed and Cured' for more on this.) It's important to incrementally improve your eating habits every year. Eventually aiming for a plant-based, whole-food diet is what I have found works best for energy healing. This lifts your energy field by simplifying and clearing the channels within you physically. Remember how we talked about channelling by simplifying and creating space? You will find the healing that takes place when you combine these cleansing, purifying practices to be rapid and profound.

Using herbs for your medicine is also important, as herbs resonate with your body naturally and have far less toxicity than conventional pharmaceuticals, or synthetic nutritional supplements. Plant medicine was also put on this Earth for us by intelligent design. This all combines, triggering a rapidly healing body.

Probably the most important principle of the Unconditional Energy Healing method is 'tuning in'. Remember that once you are tuned in, by practising meditation daily, and resonate on the same wavelength as the universal source of unconditional love, you need make no effort, and the energy will automatically be with you. Let go of your ego, including your past beliefs, attitudes and opinions; simplify your life, your food and your mind, and you will become an open channel. Healing will then take place effortlessly. Humility and gratitude are golden keys. All will be provided from above, by grace.

I will leave you with these closing thoughts. There is indeed a great universal intelligence that lies behind this visible three-dimensional world, which is constantly and infinitely pouring out the knowledge, information and the energy we need to grow, progress and heal. It is all encompassed within the love that we share for each other, our family, our children and our spouse. The love for a newborn family member could possibly be the closest we come to switching on 100 per cent to this healing energy.

Just as white light can be broken into millions of colours, the unconditional, universal love I have called 'unconditional healing energy' contains all the millions of pieces of information we could ever need to

be whole, healed, and all we can potentially be. It is infinitely ours to freely receive, and share.

As you become more and more familiar with the principles and practices found in this book, you will receive an ever-increasing presence, as a soft, peaceful, warm glow within. You will know that you are loved and supported by a benevolent loving intelligence that is always there for you, and only requires you to be on the same page, with absolute truth in your mind. May you continually receive a stream of life-giving energy from above.

There will surely be some interesting times ahead, so persistence and discipline will be needed, but with this knowledge, may your journey be filled with joy and happiness.

Many blessings,
Brett.

Unconditional Energy Healing – Training Workshops

You can learn how to practise Unconditional Energy Healing directly from Brett in person. Brett offers training workshops in Unconditional Energy Healing as a certificate course. These courses are held around New Zealand and elsewhere.

To find out more visit **www.brettelliott.com/events**.

Other publications

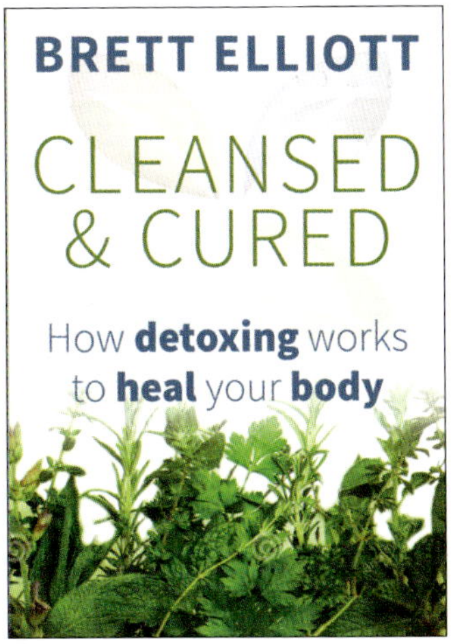

Cleansed & Cured
How detoxing works to heal your body
Published 2018
978-1-86953-983-2

Toxic overload is the single biggest and most lethal health epidemic of our time, and yet it's rarely spoken about. Now, at last, there is a clear explanation of how chronic toxicity is underlying the most common ailments in the developed world. Find out how a simple, natural inner-body cleansing programme can reduce the chronic inflammation in your body that underlies so many of today's health problems, including allergies, arthritis, asthma, bloating, coeliac disease, Crohn's disease, constipation, diverticulitis, eczema, fatigue, gout, high blood pressure, high blood sugar, high cholesterol, irritable bowel, memory loss, palpitations, psoriasis, reflux, sinusitis, ulcers, weight gain. Brett Elliot's realistic and practical advice will guide you to better health and wellbeing through understanding what is really behind many of these. His book includes detox diet recipes, along with other healing methods to help your body, and the latest information supported by hundreds of scientific references.

References

Introduction

1 Clara Moskowitz, 'What's 96 Percent of the Universe Made Of? Astronomers Don't Know', accessed on 26 May 2021, https://www.space.com/11642-dark-matter-dark-energy-4-percent-universe-panek.html.

2 Michael Marshall, 'The secret of how life on earth began', 31 October 2016, http://www.bbc.com/earth/story/20161026-the-secret-of-how-life-on-earth-began.

3 Oliver Burkeman, 'Why can't the world's greatest minds solve the mystery of consciousness?', 21 January 2015, https://www.theguardian.com/science/2015/jan/21/-sp-why-cant-worlds-greatest-minds-solve-mystery-consciousness; Tanya Lewis, 'Scientists closing in on theory of consciousness', accessed on 26 May 2021, https://www.livescience.com/47096-theories-seek-to-explain-consciousness.html.

4 David Nield, '99% of The Microbes in Our Own Bodies Are Still a Total Mystery to Science', 25 August 2017, https://www.sciencealert.com/more-than-99-percent-of-the-microbes-inside-us-are-unknown-to-science.

5 National Oceanic and Atmospheric Administration, US Dept of Commerce 'How much of the ocean have we explored?', 26 February 2021, https://oceanservice.noaa.gov/facts/exploration.html.

6 Ibid.

7 Ibid.

Chapter 1: A higher perspective

1 Belief — noun. 1. Something believed; an opinion or conviction: a belief that the earth is flat; 2. Confidence in the truth or existence of something not immediately susceptible to rigorous proof: a statement unworthy of belief; 3. Confidence; faith; trust: a child's belief in his parents; 4. A religious tenet or tenets; religious creed or faith: the Christian belief. http://www.dictionary.com/browse/beliefs.
Attitude — noun. 1. Manner, disposition, feeling, position, etc., with regard to a person or thing; tendency or orientation, especially of the mind: a negative attitude; group attitudes; 2. Position or posture of the body appropriate to or expressive of an action, emotion, etc.: a threatening attitude; a relaxed attitude. http://www.dictionary.com/browse/attitude?s=t.
Opinion — noun. 1. A belief or judgment that rests on grounds insufficient to produce complete certainty; 2. A personal view, attitude, or appraisal. http://www.dictionary.com/browse/opinion?s=t.

2 Wikipedia, 'Ego', accessed on 26 May 2021, https://en.wikipedia.org/wiki/Id,_ego_and_super-ego#Ego.

3 Wikipedia, 'Super-ego', accessed 26 May 2021, https://en.wikipedia.org/wiki/Id,_ego_and_super-ego#Super-ego.

4 Wikipedia, 'Overview effect', accessed 26 May 2021, https://en.wikipedia.org/wiki/Overview_effect.

Chapter 2: Energy exchange

1 Encyclopaedia Britannica, 'Conservation law', *Encyclopaedia Britannica*, 26 April 2021, https://www.britannica.com/science/conservation-law
2 Jesse Emspak, 13 April 2016, 'What Will Happen to Earth When the Sun Dies?' https://www.livescience.com/32879-what-happens-to-earth-when-sun-dies.html.

Chapter 3: What is healing energy?

1 Bruce Lipton, PhD, 'The Jump From Cell Culture to Consciousness', Integ Med (Encinitas), December 2017, 16(6): 44–50, https://www.ncbi.nlm.nih.gov/pmc/articles/PMC6438088/; Evangelia Tzika, et al., 'Epigenetics and Metabolism in Health and Disease', Front Genet, 2018; 9: 361, https://www.ncbi.nlm.nih.gov/pmc/articles/PMC6153363/.
2 National Research Council, 'Plasma Physics of the Local Cosmos', Washington DC, The National Academies Press, 2004, https://www.nap.edu/catalog/10993/plasma-physics-of-the-local-cosmos; NASA, 'Tour of the Electromagnetic Spectrum: Microwave', last updated 15 June 2021, https://science.nasa.gov/ems/06_microwaves.
3 Xu Yan, et al., 'Plasma medicine for neuroscience — an introduction', Chinese Neurosurgical Journal, 2019, 5(25), https://cnjournal.biomedcentral.com/articles/10.1186/s41016-019-0172-9.
4 Ibid.
5 'Omnipotent, Omniscient and Omnipresent God: Definition & Overview', study.com, accessed 4 July 2021, https://study.com/academy/lesson/omnipotent-omniscient-and-omnipresent-god-definition-lesson-quiz.html.

Chapter 5: Connecting

1 Stanford Encyclopedia of Philosophy, 'Nonexistent Objects', 22 August 2006; revised 19 March 2019, https://plato.stanford.edu/entries/nonexistent-objects/.
2 Reena Mukamal, American Academy of Opthamology, 'How Humans see in Color', 8 June 2017, https://www.aao.org/eye-health/tips-prevention/how-humans-see-in-color.

Chapter 6: Tapping in

1 Ali Sundermier, '99.9999999% of Your Body Is Empty Space', 23 September 2016, https://www.sciencealert.com/99-9999999-of-your-body-is-empty-space.
2 J S Farnes, 'A unifying theory of dark energy and dark matter: Negative masses and matter creation within a modified ΛCDM framework', *Astronomy & Astrophysics*, 620, December 2018, https://www.aanda.org/articles/aa/full_html/2018/12/aa32898-18/aa32898-18.html.
3 Hari Sharma, 'Meditation: Process and effects', Ayu, July–September 2015; 36(3): 233–37, https://www.ncbi.nlm.nih.gov/pmc/articles/PMC4895748/; Cosimo Urgesi (ed.), 'Future directions in meditation research: Recommendations for expanding the field of contemplative science' *PLoS One*, 2018; 13(11): e0205740, https://www.ncbi.nlm.nih.gov/pmc/articles/PMC6221271/; Fadel Zeidan and David Vago, 'Mindfulness meditation-based pain relief: a mechanistic account', *Ann N Y Acad Sci.*, June 2016; 1373(1): 114–27, https://www.ncbi.nlm.nih.gov/pmc/articles/PMC4941786/; Sara Wagner Robb, et al., 'Mindfulness-based stress reduction teachers, practice characteristics, cancer incidence, and health: a nationwide ecological description', *BMC Complement Altern Med*, 2015; 15: 24, https://www.ncbi.nlm.nih.gov/pmc/articles/PMC4342874/; Elissa Epel et al., 'Can meditation slow rate of cellular aging? Cognitive stress, mindfulness, and telomeres', *Ann N Y Acad Sci*, August 2009; 1172: 34–53, https://www.ncbi.nlm.nih.gov/pmc/articles/PMC3057175/

4 Jeanne Ball, 'Could Meditation Have Something to Do with Plummeting Crime Rates?' 27 November 2010; updated 17 November 2011, https://www.huffpost.com/entry/a-thanksgiving-blessing-f_b_788053.
5 Christopher Timmerman et al., 'DMT Models the Near-Death Experience', *Front Psychol.*, 2018; 9: 1424, https://www.ncbi.nlm.nih.gov/pmc/articles/PMC6107838/.
6 Steven A. Barker, 'N, N-Dimethyltryptamine (DMT), an Endogenous Hallucinogen: Past, Present, and Future Research to Determine Its Role and Function' *Front Neurosci*, 2018; 12: 536, https://www.ncbi.nlm.nih.gov/pmc/articles/PMC6088236/.
7 Tanuj Dada et al., 'Mindfulness Meditation Reduces Intraocular Pressure, Lowers Stress Biomarkers and Modulates Gene Expression in Glaucoma: a randomized controlled trial', *J Glaucoma,* December 2018; 27(12): 1061–67, https://pubmed.ncbi.nlm.nih.gov/30256277/.

Chapter 7: The simplicity principle

1 Steven Allender, et al, 'Quantifying Urbanization as a Risk Factor for Noncommunicable Disease', *J Urban Health*, October 2011; 88(5): 906–18, https://www.ncbi.nlm.nih.gov/pmc/articles/PMC3191205/; K. Steyn, et al., 'Urbanization and the risk for chronic diseases of lifestyle in the black population of the Cape Peninsula, South Africa', *J Cardiovasc Risk*, April 1997; 4(2):135–42, https://www.ncbi.nlm.nih.gov/pubmed/9304495

Chapter 8: Channelling space

1 'Homeostasis', *Encyclopedia Britannica*, 27 May 2020, https://www.britannica.com/science/homeostasis.
2 NASA, 'Tests of Big Bang: The CMB', 9 May 2016, https://wmap.gsfc.nasa.gov/universe/bb_tests_cmb.html.
3 Rainee N. Simons et al., 'Demonstration of Multi-Gbps Data Rates at Ka-Band Using Software-Defined Modem and Broadband High Power Amplifier for Space Communications', 1 April 2011, https://ntrs.nasa.gov/archive/nasa/casi.ntrs.nasa.gov/20110012462.pdf.
4 Wikipedia, 'Conservation of energy', last edited 11 June 2021, https://en.wikipedia.org/wiki/Conservation_of_energy.

Chapter 9: The mind

1 National Human Genome Research Institute, 'Chromosomes Fact Sheet', last updated 15 August 2020, https://www.genome.gov/about-genomics/fact-sheets/Chromosomes-Fact-Sheet.
2 Soujanya Vinayagamurthy et al, 'Extra-telomeric impact of telomeres: Emerging molecular connections in pluripotency or stemness', Biol Chem, July 2020; 295(30): 10245–54, https://pubmed.ncbi.nlm.nih.gov/32444498/; Christopher Tiommerman et al., 'DMT Models the Near-Death Experience', Front Psychol, 2018; 9: 1424, https://www.ncbi.nlm.nih.gov/pmc/articles/PMC6107838/.
3 Julie A. Segre, National Human Genome Research Institute, 'Telomere', https://www.genome.gov/genetics-glossary/Telomere.
4 Marta Alda et al., 'Zen meditation, Length of Telomeres, and the Role of Experiential Avoidance and Compassion', *Mindfulness (NY)*, 2016; 7: 651–59, https://www.ncbi.nlm.nih.gov/pmc/articles/PMC4859856/.

Chapter 10: Using your hands

1 University of California — Davis, 'Sixth sense: How do we sense electric fields?' *ScienceDaily*, 13 October 2015, https://www.sciencedaily.com/releases/2015/10/151013112134.htm.

Chapter 11: Healing yourself

1 Shamini Jain, et al, 'Clinical Studies of Biofield Therapies: Summary, Methodological Challenges, and Recommendations', *Glob Adv Health Med*, November 2015; 4(Suppl): 58–66, https://www.ncbi.nlm.nih.gov/pmc/articles/PMC4654788/.

2 Pamela J Potter, 'Energy therapies in advanced practice oncology: an evidence-informed practice approach', *J Adv Pract Oncol*, May 2013; 4(3): 139–51, https://pubmed.ncbi.nlm.nih.gov/25031994/.
3 World Health Organization, 'Radiation: electromagnetic fields' Q&A.
4 'Magnetic resonance', *Encyclopedia Britannica*, 25 January 2011, https://www.britannica.com/science/magnetic-resonance.
5 Jeffrey Long, 'Near-Death Experiences Evidence for Their Reality', *Mo Med*, September–October 2014; 111(5): 372–80, https://www.ncbi.nlm.nih.gov/pmc/articles/PMC6172100/.
6 Chang-Hwan Im et al,'Recent advances in biomagnetism and its applications', *Biomed Eng Lett*, August 2017; 7(3): 183–84, https://www.ncbi.nlm.nih.gov/pmc/articles/PMC6208498/.
7 World Health Organization, 'Radiation: electromagnetic fields' Q&A, 4 August 2016, https://www.who.int/peh-emf/about/WhatisEMF/en/.
8 Conrad Hackett and David McClendon, 'Christians remain world's largest religious group, but they are declining in Europe', Pew Research Center, 5 April 2017, https://www.pewresearch.org/fact-tank/2017/04/05/christians-remain-worlds-largest-religious-group-but-they-are-declining-in-europe/.
9 George B Stefano, 'DNA MemoChip: Long-Term and High Capacity Information Storage and Select Retrieval', *Med Sci Monit*, 2018; 24: 1185–87, https://www.ncbi.nlm.nih.gov/pmc/articles/PMC5841191/.
10 Boeing, 'World Class Supplier Quality', accessed on 16 June 2021, https://787updates.newairplane.com/787-Suppliers/World-Class-Supplier-Quality#.
11 US National Library of Medicine, 'What is DNA?', Medline Plus, last reviewed 19 January 2021, https://medlineplus.gov/genetics//understanding/basics/dna.
12 US National Library of Medicine, 'What is noncoding DNA?', Medline Plus, last reviewed 19 January 2021, https://ghr.nlm.nih.gov/primer/basics/noncodingdna.
13 Nobel Prize, press release, 3 October 2016, https://www.nobelprize.org/prizes/medicine/2016/press-release/; L Gaman et al., 'Can ageing be slowed? Hormetic and redox perspectives', *J Med Life*, 14 November 2011; 4(4): 346–51, https://www.ncbi.nlm.nih.gov/pmc/articles/PMC3227150/; Petric Kuballa et al., 'Autophagy and the Immune System', *Annual Review of Immunology*, April 2012; 30: 611–46, https://www.annualreviews.org/doi/10.1146/annurev-immunol-020711-074948; Long, 'Near-Death Experiences Evidence for Their Reality'.
14 Ali Sundermier, '99.9999999% of Your Body Is Empty Space'.
15 Interagency Working Group on the Physics of the Universe, National Science and Technology Council Committee on Science, 'A 21st Century Frontier for Discovery: The Physics of the Universe', February 2004, https://pcos.gsfc.nasa.gov/docs/Physics_of_the_Universe.pdf.
16 Ethan Siegel, 'How Far is the Edge of the Universe?', *Science & Nonduality*, accessed on 16 June 2021, https://www.scienceandnonduality.com/article/how-far-is-the-edge-of-the-universe.
17 Interagency Working Group on the Physics of the Universe, National Science and Technology Council Committee on Science, 'A 21st Century Frontier for Discovery: The Physics of the Universe'.
18 Wikipedia, 'Cosmic dust', last updated 21 June 2021, https://en.wikipedia.org/wiki/Cosmic_dust.
19 Tiara Dillworth et al, 'Neurophysiology of pain and hypnosis for chronic pain', *Transl Behav Med*, March 2012; 2(1): 65–72, https://www.ncbi.nlm.nih.gov/pmc/articles/PMC3717822/.
20 Mark P Jensen and David R Patterson, 'Hypnotic Approaches for Chronic Pain Management', *Am Psychol*, February–March 2014; 69(2): 167–77, https://

www.ncbi.nlm.nih.gov/pmc/articles/PMC4465776/.

21 Ben Colagiuri et al, 'The placebo effect: from concepts to genes', *Neuroscience*, 29 October 2015; 307: 171–90, https://www.ncbi.nlm.nih.gov/pmc/articles/PMC5367890/.

22 Luana Colloca and Franklin G Miller, 'The nocebo effect and its relevance for clinical practice', *Psychosom Med*, September 2011; 73(7): 598–603, https://www.ncbi.nlm.nih.gov/pmc/articles/PMC3167012/.

23 Isabelle Mansuy and Safa Mohanna, 'Epigenetics and the Human Brain: Where Nurture Meets Nature', *Cerebrum*, May–June 2011; 2011: 8, https://www.ncbi.nlm.nih.gov/pmc/articles/PMC3574773/.

Epilogue: The healing journey begins

1 Anthony Trewavas, 'Green Plants as Intelligent Organisms', *Trends Plant Sci*, September 2005; 10(9): 413–9, https://pubmed.ncbi.nlm.nih.gov/16054860/; Daniela Pinto and Thorsten Mascher, '(Actino)Bacterial "Intelligence": Using Comparative Genomics to Unravel the Information Processing Capacities of Microbes', *Curr Genet*, August 2016; 62(3): 487–98, https://pubmed.ncbi.nlm.nih.gov/26852121/.

2 Robert S Bobrow, 'Evidence for a Communal Consciousness', *Explore (NY)*, July–August 2011; 7(4): 246–8, https://pubmed.ncbi.nlm.nih.gov/21724158/.

3 Matt Williams, 'A universe of 10 dimensions', *Universe Today*, 11 December 2014, https://phys.org/news/2014-12-universe-dimensions.html.